Children's Folklore

Children's Folklore

A Handbook

Elizabeth Tucker

Greenwood Folklore Handbooks

GREENWOOD PRESS
Westport, Connecticut • London

Library of Congress Cataloging-in-Publication Data

Tucker, Elizabeth, 1948–
    Children's folklore : a handbook / Elizabeth Tucker.
        p. cm. — (Greenwood folklore handbooks, ISSN 1549–733X)
    Includes bibliographical references and index.
    ISBN: 978–0–313–34189–2 (alk. paper)
1. Folklore and children—Handbooks, manuals, etc.   2. Children—
Folklore—Handbooks, manuals, etc.   I. Title.
GR43.C4T83   2008
398.2083—dc22   2008019925

British Library Cataloguing in Publication Data is available.

Library of Congress Catalog Card Number: 2008019925
ISBN: 978–0–313–34189–2
ISSN: 1549–733X

First published in 2008

Greenwood Press, 88 Post Road West, Westport, CT 06881
An imprint of Greenwood Publishing Group, Inc.
www.greenwood.com

Printed in the United States of America

∞™

The paper used in this book complies with the
Permanent Paper Standard issued by the National
Information Standards Organization (Z39.48–1984).

10   9   8   7   6   5   4   3   2   1

Copyright Acknowledgments

Excerpts from Bill Ellis, "'Ralph and Rudy': The Audience Role in
Recreating a Campus Legend," *Western Folklore* 51.3 (July 1982): 173–74.
Western States Folklore Society © 1982. Reprinted with permission.

Contents

Preface

L ike other researchers in the field of children's folklore, I have enjoyed discovering the remarkable range of children's traditions. Children demonstrate their creativity by coming up with new versions of old rhymes, songs, narratives, and other expressive forms; they also tend to preserve certain patterns that have pleased previous generations of young people. While doing research for this book, I have collected legends and songs that resembled the ones I learned as a child in the 1950s and 1960s. I have also learned that my students, who have grown up in a world different from the one I knew during childhood, have cherished some of the same traditions, including making forts out of couch cushions and playing games on neighborhood streets.

This handbook provides an overview of children's folklore since the late 1800s, with particular attention to material that has emerged since the publication of relatively recent analytical surveys of children's folklore: *Children's Folklore: A Source Book,* edited by Brian Sutton-Smith, Jay Mechling, Thomas W. Johnson, and Felicia R. McMahon (1995) and *American Children's Folklore* by Simon J. Bronner (1988). Since the handbook cannot cover all children's folklore, it offers texts that represent major genres and areas of study. Most examples and texts come from English-speaking countries, but some come from other parts of the world.

The first chapter of this handbook traces the development of children's folklore study from the late nineteenth century to the early twenty-first century, with attention to reflections of social and political change and connections between children's folklore and education. Chapter 1 also examines issues related to fieldwork with children. Chapter 2 defines key terms, including those that identify genres of children's folklore. Examples and texts appear in chapter 3, which provides contextual information for each item of folklore. Chapter 4 covers children's folklore scholarship from its earliest days to our current era, and chapter 5 puts children's folklore in the contexts of literature, films, television, and mass-produced dolls, toys, and games. The bibliography and list of Internet resources at the end of the book give the reader enough resources to begin children's folklore research.

I would like to thank the many kind people who have helped me find information and texts for this handbook. Among them are Kelly Armor at the Erie Art Museum, Simon J. Bronner at Penn State Harrisburg, Carole Carpenter at York University, Irene Chagall of the Center for Folklife and Cultural Heritage at the Smithsonian Institution, Pamela Dean at the Northeast Folklore Archive of the University of Maine, Bill Ellis at Penn State Hazleton, June Factor at the University of Melbourne, Janet Gilmore at the University of Wisconsin–Madison, Diane Goldstein at Memorial University at Newfoundland, Janet Langlois at Wayne State University, John McDowell at Indiana University, Richard March of the Wisconsin Arts Board, W.F.H. Nicolaisen at the University of Aberdeen, Elliott Oring, Azizi Powell of Cocojams.com, Kelly Revak at the University of California at Berkeley, Karen Prowda, M.D., Jan Rosenberg of the Folklore and Education section of the American Folklore Society, Brian Sutton-Smith, J.D.A. Widdowson at the University of Sheffield, Randy Williams at the Fife Folklore Archive of Utah State University, and Peggy Yocom at George Mason University. Faye McMahon at Syracuse University deserves particular thanks for her generosity in offering books and helpful insights. I also want to thank my father, Frank H. Tucker, my sisters, Sarah Owens and Margaret Mitchell, and my cousins, Linda Faatz, John Treworgy, and Susie and James Whalen. One son, Peter Gould, taught me numerous songs, rhymes, and games; the others, Tom Gould and Chris Powell, also taught me many things, and so did my granddaughter Emilie and students in my folklore classes. I also want to thank the Maerz family for their help and friendship.

Special thanks go to the photographers who took the wonderful pictures included in this book: Martha Cooper, Martha Harris, Buzz Hays, and my husband, Geoffrey Gould, whose support made a big difference at every stage of this book's preparation. Lastly, I want to thank my editor, George Butler, who has made Greenwood's Folklore Handbooks such a fine and useful series.

One

Introduction

LIGHT AS A FEATHER...

Six children kneel on the floor of a school band room. Each child holds two fingers under the torso of a friend who lies at the center of their group. In unison, the six children chant "Light as a feather, stiff as a board. Light as a feather, stiff as a board." After 20 seconds of chanting, a monster's face with horrible white eyes makes the children scream. Twenty-four seconds after its beginning, the performance abruptly ends.

This performance of levitation, a ritual that takes place during children's sleepovers, campouts, and other get-togethers, appeared in a brief video on the Internet's YouTube in October 2006. Seven months later, when I watched the video, 4,424 others had already seen it. This is a good example of children's folklore: traditional knowledge shared by a group of two or more children, usually without involvement by adults. Some children's folklore has circulated for centuries. Samuel Pepys described four French girls performing levitation in his diary in 1665 (Latham and Matthews 177–78). Since then, the childhood underground—a network of children that transmits children's folklore, with creative variations—has kept levitation alive. For many years, few adults noticed children lifting each other late at night, but now levitation belongs to the constantly changing stream of video culture. Contemporary technology has made it possible for children to broadcast their own videos of levitation and other kinds of folklore to a limitless audience of children and adults that can offer comments, criticism, and videos of similar material.

Internet technology offers just one of many expressions of the rich array of games, songs, rhymes, jokes, riddles, tales, legends, pranks, toys, and other amusements

Teenagers in Maine practice the ritual of levitation in the summer of 2007. Photograph by Martha Harris.

that comprise children's folklore. Study of this field began in the late nineteenth century, when scholars began to record and analyze children's games and songs in England and the United States. After the British scholars Iona and Peter Opie published their groundbreaking *Lore and Language of Schoolchildren* in 1959, a new era of children's folklore study began. The most recent book-length surveys and analyses of children's folklore have been *American Children's Folklore* by Simon J. Bronner (1988) and *Children's Folklore: A Source Book,* edited by Brian Sutton-Smith, Jay Mechling, Thomas W. Johnson, and Felicia R. McMahon (1995). The present handbook attempts to bring children's folklore study up to date, with a sampling of representative texts and an overview of scholarship. The range of material covered here does not diverge radically from that of other recent surveys, but it puts more emphasis on nature lore and imaginative, dangerous, and sexually oriented games than some other surveys have done. Like other children's folklore surveys, this one includes material gathered from children at school and in their home neighborhoods. Many examples come from countries where people speak English; non-English examples appear in translation.

Children's folklore, created and shared by children, differs from folklore *for* children, sometimes called nursery lore, which adults deem suitable for the young.

The clapping game Pat-a-cake, for example, comes from British oral tradition of the seventeenth century. Parents teach this game to their young children (Opie and Opie, *Oxford Dictionary* 341–42). When children grow old enough to play with each other, they learn games and rhymes that do not come from adults. One popular rhyme, for example, includes the lines "Boys are rotten, made out of cotton / Girls are sexy, made out of Pepsi" (see chapter 3 for the rhyme's full text). Parents and other adults would not generally teach children this rhyme, which represents girls' increasing awareness of boys. Because the rhyme has subversive appeal, it moves rapidly from one group of children to another.

In contrast to children, who respond to their peer groups' traditions, some adults seem minimally aware of this kind of communication: a strange situation, since these adults were once children themselves. In "Psychology of Children," Brian Sutton-Smith coined the term *triviality barrier* for adults' insensitivity to children's folklore. If adults view children's pursuits as trivial, they will make little effort to understand them. Part of this attitude comes from adults' reluctance to accept children's enjoyment of subversive, ribald, dangerous, and otherwise unacceptable material that teachers and parents would not usually recommend. Striving to teach children to be good, productive citizens, teachers and parents may forget that they once participated in subversive activities themselves.

Adults who observe their children closely, however, gain considerable respect for their youngsters' communication skills. Recently I heard about an American couple who traveled to Kazakhstan to adopt a child, bringing along their eight-year-old son, Stephen. While waiting for the adoption to be finalized, the parents took Stephen out to play in a park. Quickly getting acquainted with several Russian children there, Stephen played Hide-and-Seek, Tag, and Leapfrog. Although the children spoke to each other in their own languages, they communicated primarily through gestures that signaled the kinds of games they wanted to play next. This interesting example reminds us that games and other nonverbal lore can circulate easily without words of explanation.

On Halloween, the joyous festival of supernatural and dramatic events that takes place on October 31, children's folklore gains adults' attention in various ways. Besides attending parties and trick-or-treat expeditions organized by adults, children create costumes, play pranks, and recite traditional demands such as "Trick or treat, smell my feet, give me something good to eat!" In some communities, a traditional "Mischief Night" the night before Halloween gives children a chance to play pranks. Some teenagers' pranks, such as dropping pumpkins off highway overpasses, cause damage and concern, but many pranks, such as soaping windows and writing rude words on streets with shaving cream, cause little trouble. Jack Santino's *Halloween and Other Festivals of Death and Life* (1994) traces the evolution of this important holiday, which allows children to express themselves rudely and exuberantly within traditional limits.

Children dressed as the Candy Corn Fairy and Harry Potter on Halloween, 2007. Photograph by Martha Harris.

TRADITION AND CREATIVITY

William Wells Newell, author of *Games and Songs of American Children* (1883), suggests that children are both conservative and creative; once they learn traditional texts, they will pass them along to others, adding some creative changes of their own. Folklore scholar Gary Alan Fine explains that "Newell's paradox"—the combination of tradition with creative variation—makes sense in terms of text, context, and performance. Texts tend to stay stable while context changes, and performance brings together imaginative and traditional elements.

Is children's folklore alive and well, or has it declined in recent years? As technological advances have moved from television to videogames, e-mail, Instant Messaging, cellular telephones, and YouTube, educators have asked whether increasing emphasis on technology is destroying young people's oral and customary traditions. David Sobel, director of teacher certification programs at the graduate school of Antioch New England in New Hampshire, expresses concern about "erosion of childhood," stating that "computers seem like a river in flood, washing away the soil that roots children to the natural world." This statement of concern is one of many that have emerged in scholarly literature and in the popular press. While these changes seem worrisome, we should keep in mind Iona and Peter Opie's explanation that "the belief that traditional games are dying out is itself traditional; it was received opinion even when those who now regret the passing of the games were themselves vigorously playing them" (*Children's Games* 14). William Wells Newell bewails the demise of children's games in his 1883 *Games and Songs of American Children,* stating that his collection represents "an expiring custom" (1). Some of this continuing concern seems to come from inevitable changes in children's play patterns. Games that we played ourselves as children may change or disappear later on; it is not easy to accept such changes.

Some contemporary folklorists have observed, however, that patterns of children's play have shifted in alarming ways. In her eloquent essay "'Our Dreams in Action': Spirituality and Children's Play Today," Carole H. Carpenter explains how much boys' involvement in hockey has changed in Canada. Instead of enjoying the folk version of hockey called Shinny, boys have been drawn into large, expensive hockey leagues organized by adults, and much of the joy of "folk hockey" has been lost. Because of such losses, Carpenter suggests that "adults must reshape their agenda for childhood by withdrawing pressures on the young to grow up, thereby allowing them to grow" (178). Similarly, Steven Zeitlin, executive director of City Lore in New York City, observes that "Parents drive children at a very young age to get them on the right track for success, so every waking moment is programmed, which doesn't leave lots of time for play" (Williams and Feldman M-25). Adults' attempts to bring back Stickball and other street games, notably in the Web site Streetplay.com (http://www.streetplay.com), have revived older forms of play to some extent. Meanwhile, children's performances of "Light As a Feather" and other forms of folklore on YouTube show that kids have been finding new ways to share traditions that interest them.

Proof that children's folklore is alive and well comes from the 2003 study *Traditional English Language Genres: Continuity and Change, 1950–2000,* by Joanne Green and J.D.A. Widdowson. Finding the dawn of a new millennium to be a good time to review recent linguistic developments, Green and Widdowson observe, "As new patterns of life and work succeed the old, so new forms of language take the place of earlier usage" (1). Their list of 50 rhymes collected from children clearly demonstrates that some rhymes have circulated more actively than others. Among the factors contributing to linguistic change, they mention political correctness and the fact that "the older patterns of rural life have changed beyond recognition" (10). Green and Widdowson conclude that change has positive effects; the "constant updating of children's rhymes, songs, and games" is "the hallmark of their extraordinary ability to survive, despite all the pressure on children to conform." New forms, such as football chants, "represent a reinvigoration of the genre as a whole" (519). This insightful and upbeat conclusion reminds us that children can adapt to change while retaining folk traditions of their own choosing.

REFLECTIONS OF SOCIAL AND POLITICAL CHANGE

Children's folklore scholarship began in the nineteenth century, when industrial growth made people think about children's expressive behavior. The first Industrial Revolution, from the late eighteenth to the early nineteenth century, inspired Europe's Romantic movement, which idealized childhood in the context of rural life, nature, and emotion. The second Industrial Revolution, from 1865 to the 1890s, involved massive growth in American industry and finance, with fast-growing railroads and increasing ethnic diversity through immigration. In his poem "My Heart Leaps Up When I Behold," William Wordsworth states, "The child is father of the man": an often-quoted line that represents nineteenth-century intellectuals' concept of children as visionaries and leaders. Alexander Chamberlain, who edited the *Journal of American Folklore* from 1900 to 1907, suggests that people profit enormously from "[childhood's] wisdom, its naiveté, its ingenuity, and its touch of divinity" (403).

The first folklorists of childhood, including Alexander Chamberlain, William Wells Newell, and Lady Alice Bertha Gomme, followed an evolutionary approach, viewing children as preservers of earlier culture and developers of creative variations. These evolution-oriented scholars believed that society moved forward through three stages: savagery, barbarism, and civilization. According to this approach, adults maintained current civilization, but children reflected civilization's earlier achievements. In his book *Folklife Studies from the Gilded Age,* Simon J. Bronner articulates the close relationship between early children's folklore studies and the focus on progress and rationality of the late nineteenth century's Gilded Age (119–34). Bronner's essay "Expressing and Creating Ourselves in Childhood" aptly compares children's folklore studies of the Gilded Age with contemporary children's folklore scholarship: "As Chamberlain and Newell used folklore research to reflect on the hierarchical industrial age rising in their Gilded Age society, so the trend today is to contemplate the swirling social currents of an electronic era. More than an objective anthropological endeavor envisioned by Chamberlain, the ethnographic task now is broadly interdisciplinary and simultaneously involves us as participants and observers" (55). Although evolutionary analysis of children's folklore has become a fossil in the archives of early scholarship, rapid social and economic change still causes excitement and concern.

After the first flowering of children's folklore scholarship in the late nineteenth century, studies of children's games, songs, and other traditions became sporadic. The upheavals of World Wars I and II and the Great Depression of the 1930s did not encourage contemplation of children's expressive culture. There were, however, some important contributions to children's folklore study, including Norman Douglas's *London Street Games* (1916/1931) and Edward Norton's *Play Streets* (1937). Some post–World War II studies record rhymes and observations of play from earlier years. In their admirably thorough *Children's Games in Street and Playground,* Iona and Peter Opie note that children incarcerated at Auschwitz during World War II played imaginative games based on the tragic events that they witnessed (331). The Opies include a number of topical rhymes from 1929 to 1958 in their canonical *Lore and Language of Schoolchildren* (1959), including songs with the first lines "Kaiser Bill went up the hill," "Roll along Mussolini, roll along," "In 1941 old Hitler ate a bun," and "Catch a falling sputnik" (98–106).

From the late 1950s to the present, scholars have kept extensive records of children's folklore. The many publications of play theorist Brian Sutton-Smith have documented children's expressive behavior in the context of social change. His book *The Folkgames of Children* (1972) includes an interesting essay on the effect of British colonialism on Maori play and games (317–30). Sutton-Smith's more recent books *Toys As Culture* (1986) and *The Ambiguity of Play* (1998) also offer important insights. Simon J. Bronner's *American Children's Folklore* (1988) offers an excellent selection of children's expressive behavior in social contexts, with particularly interesting samples of material culture. For more details on the work of Sutton-Smith, Bronner, and other scholars of the late twentieth and twenty-first century, see chapters 2 and 4.

During the 1960s, the hippie movement and demonstrations against the Vietnam War reminded Americans of young people's power to disrupt adults' social and political structures. After this period of unrest, traditional restrictions on college students' behavior loosened on most campuses, and scholars with an interest in children's and adolescents' behavior took a closer look at young people's subversive behavior. Mary and Herbert Knapp devote chapter 4 of their *One Potato, Two Potato: The Secret Education of American Children* (1976) to "resistance," including parodies and shockers. Josepha Sherman and T.K.F. Weisskopf's *Greasy Grimy Gopher Guts: The Subversive Folklore of Childhood* (1995) celebrates children's joyful inversion of adults' rules. Performance theorists from the late 1960s to more recent times have examined children's power dynamics in detail (see chapter 4).

Since the late 1980s, major changes have taken place in the world. Some of these changes have been political: the Berlin Wall came down in 1989, the Soviet Union collapsed in 1991, and civil war in northern Africa caused massive dislocation of children and their parents in the early 1990s. Folklorists have documented the effects of some of these changes on children's folklore. Marjatta Kalliala's *Play Culture in a Changing World* (2006) cites Margarita Lioubart's research in Russian day-care centers in the early 1990s, when Power Rangers and Barbies took the place of governmentally sanctioned "militia play" (24). Felicia R. McMahon's insightful *Not Just Child's Play: Emerging Tradition and the Lost Boys of Sudan* (2007) explores how DiDinga youths who immigrated from the Sudan to Syracuse playfully use songs, dances, and art forms learned in childhood as strategies for adaptation to their new lives in the United States. Rather than viewing themselves as victims, these young men take pride in sharing and preserving DiDinga culture through public performances and gatherings with fellow refugees. McMahon's book provides a model for further folkloristic studies of displaced children's adjustment through performance of cherished folk traditions.

In their 1995 essay "The Past in the Present: Theoretical Directions for Children's Folklore," Felicia R. McMahon and Brian Sutton-Smith ask "how it is that our adult culture so typically suppresses the power-related aspects of children's lives" (308). Unfortunately, the massacre of 12 students and a teacher at Columbine High School in Littleton, Colorado, in 1999 showed everyone how suddenly children could turn on each other and their teachers, with resultant loss of life. Since Columbine, teachers and administrators have feared sudden outbreaks of violence at school. Most school shootings have taken place in high schools, but some have occurred in middle schools and elementary schools. In 2002 the *Children's Folklore Review* devoted a special issue to the implications and effects of the Columbine massacre. Several essays in that issue are discussed in chapter 4.

Further anxiety has resulted from terrorist attacks on the United States on September 11, 2001. Before that date, American children and their parents felt relatively safe from attack within their nation's borders. As in the aftermath of other stressful events, children's play has mirrored the difficulty of both children's and adults' adjustment to a change in worldview caused by unexpected violence.

Also noteworthy have been effects of the political correctness and risk-management trends from the 1980s to the early twenty-first century. Efforts to eradicate racism and facilitate fairness to all have influenced people's attitudes toward some kinds of children's folklore. Jokes that disparage certain ethnic groups and rhymes that include derogatory terms have fallen into disfavor. Since the advent of Anti-Social Behaviour Orders in England in 1999, police have ordered children to stop playing noisy ball games; earlier, some British schools outlawed conker (chestnut) battles, jump ropes, and paper airplanes because children might get hurt while playing with them. Conn and Hal Igguldens's *The Dangerous Book for Boys* (2007) has provided a counterweight to political correctness and judicial control, explaining how to play with conkers, slingshots, and other "dangerous" things. This book's best-selling status in both England and the United States shows how exciting old-fashioned games and playthings can seem when adults limit children's entertainment. Similar accolades have greeted Andrea J. Buchanan and Miriam Peskowitz's *The Daring Book for Girls* (2007).

Other changes in the world since 1988 have been economic and technological. Since the rise of the Internet in 1991, people have radically changed how they do business and communicate with each other. Thomas L. Friedman's perceptive study *The World Is Flat* (2007) explains that the availability of cheap, instantaneous communication has made nations part of a closely connected realm. Technology specialists for Internet problems may not live anywhere near their customers; for example, a woman having problems with her Internet connection in Peoria, Illinois, may receive a solution from a technician in Bombay, India. Globalization of the world's economy has profoundly influenced people's expectations.

Children's folklore has always reflected adult society, and it has certainly shown the influence of rapid changes in communications and marketing. One case in point is the development of legends and beliefs about the dangers of drinking Coca Cola and eating candy that seems to cause an explosion. In the 1960s and 1970s, children told each other that placing a tooth in a glass of Coke would result in the tooth's disintegration. L. Michael Bell's essay "Cokelore" (1979) lists beliefs that Coke corrodes teeth and, in combination with aspirin, upsets stomachs; Gary Alan Fine's essay "Folklore Diffusion through Interactive Social Networks" (1979) documents preadolescents' legends about deaths as a result of eating Pop Rocks candy. Now such legends and beliefs have taken a new turn; kids tell each other that a combination of Diet Coke and Mentos mints will cause a huge explosion, as discussed by Trevor Blank. While this legend resembles the Pop Rocks legend, its transmission works differently. Besides hearing about Coke and Mentos in day-to-day conversation, kids watch combustible mixtures of these two ingredients on the television show *Mythbusters;* they also watch segments of this show on the Internet. Any individual who has made a video of exploding Coke and Mentos can post the video on YouTube, where people find it quickly and easily. The most popular videos show huge jets of Coke exploding into high columns, which may reflect concern about terrorism; then again, they may simply show that young people (and some older folks as well) enjoy turning quiet bottles of Coke into impressive displays of chemical power.

COLLECTING FOLKLORE FROM CHILDREN

When folklorists collect information, they carefully consider their informants' rights. Folklore fieldwork manuals, including Kenneth S. Goldstein's *Guide for Field Workers in Folklore* (1964) and Bruce Jackson's *Fieldwork* (1987), have urged folklorists to conduct their research ethically. Jackson emphasizes the importance of the "golden rule": never do anything to other people that you would not want others to do to you. Respect for other people matters more than the need to collect data. This point comes through clearly in the book *People Studying People* by Robert A. Georges and Michael Owen Jones: "fieldworker and subject are first and foremost human beings" (3).

Since the late 1970s, regulations for the protection of human research subjects have influenced folklorists' work with their informants. The American Folklore Society issued a "Statement on Ethics" in 1986 and has continued to debate issues related to ethics. Currently, the American Folklore Society's human subjects position statement specifies that folklore research "is not quantitative but overwhelmingly qualitative." Research restrictions suitable for biomedical, clinical, and experimental models are not appropriate for folklore fieldwork, which relies on trust, involvement in the local community, and protection of informants' confidentiality. According to the American Folklore Society's "Human Subjects Position Statement," folklore research that fits human subjects regulations should be eligible for expedited review.

Children deserve special consideration, because they are not yet mature enough to give informed consent to researchers. Although their parents and teachers can speak for the children to some extent, it is difficult to know whether children will, as adults, agree that they should have participated in research to which they agreed as children. Most folklore fieldworkers who have worked with children have kept the children's names confidential and changed identifying details.

Iona and Peter Opie, whose *Lore and Language of School Children* (1959) inspired many others to study children's folklore, visited playgrounds to observe children at play and to talk with the children about their games, customs, beliefs, and other forms of folklore. Identifying the children by age and gender only, the Opies preserved their informants' confidentiality. Similarly, Mary and Herbert Knapp, authors of *One Potato, Two Potato: The Secret Education of American Children* (1976), collected folklore from many different groups of children and refrained from identifying the children by name. Brian Sutton-Smith, author of *The Folkgames of Children* (1972), visited many playgrounds and schools in New Zealand and the United States. The fieldwork for Sutton-Smith's important study of children's narrative patterns, *The Folkstories of Children* (1981), took place in schools, with graduate students assisting in the process of story collection. Like the Opies and the Knapps, Sutton-Smith carefully preserved the confidentiality of the children with whom he and his assistants worked.

Since the mid-1980s, heightened concern about children's safety and well-being has caused reconsideration of young people's rights and needs. The United Nations General Assembly adopted its Convention on the Rights of the Child in 1989. Writers of books and articles on the subject of children's rights have explored why children need special consideration. Publications such as Philip Alston, Stephen Parker, and John Seymour's *Children, Rights, and the Law* (1992), F. Paul Kurmay's "Do Children Need a Bill of Rights?" (1996), and Lee E. Teitelbaum's "Children's Rights and the Problem of Equal Respect" (1999) have asked what new laws may be needed.

In this era of rapidly transmitted news, people learn very quickly about transgressions against the young. Public awareness of criminals' mistreatment of children has created a climate of fear. American school programs on "stranger danger," AMBER alerts for kidnapped children, and strict regulation of people authorized to pick children up from day care and school remind us of children's vulnerability to danger. Although these reminders help to keep children safe, they also make parents and teachers worry. Unstructured playtime outdoors, which children took for granted in the 1950s and 1960s, has, in many cases, been replaced by structured settings for supervised play.

At schools and in other structured environments such as summer camps, fieldworkers can work effectively with children. It is important to ask officials at schools or other places for permission before fieldwork begins. In any fieldwork situation, researchers must give children time to get accustomed to their visitors and ask children for their assent. Gary Alan Fine's "Methodological Problems of Collecting Folklore from Children" (1995) covers these issues in detail. Many British and American researchers have recently collected folklore from children on playgrounds and in other institutional settings. British folklorists' play audits have yielded important sources of information about children's play patterns.

For collectors of children's folklore, the Internet offers exciting potential for gathering texts and information. Karen Ellis's National Children's Folksong Repository Web site (http://www.edu-cyberpg.com/NCFR/ NCFR2.html) encourages people to submit folk songs, jump-rope chants, circle games, call-and-response songs, and other materials by using their iPods, MP3 players, and Macintosh computers or PCs. Ellis provides a toll-free telephone number that contributors can access from anywhere in the United States. Emphasizing the importance of preserving traditional material, she asks each visitor to her Web site to "sing or chant [a song]. Save it now!" Her efforts have resulted in an overflowing archive of material that offers resources for future researchers.

FOLKLORE AND EDUCATION

Children's folklore educates young people in important ways. The pioneering American folklorist Dorothy Howard learned about children's folklore in the 1930s while teaching at a New York public school. She observed that her immigrant students were "learning English from each other on the playground faster than from their text books and from [her] in the classroom." This realization resulted in collections of American and Australian children's folklore that have inspired later fieldworkers to make similar efforts. For more details on Howard's work, see chapters 4 and 5.

According to Richard Bauman, "the most significant potential contribution that the close study of children's folklore can make is in revealing the truly impressive range of linguistic and sociolinguistic competencies that is fostered by the children's own peer group culture" (184). Besides linguistic skills, many other kinds of expertise grow through children's interaction. The childhood underground functions so efficiently that adults may not know much about their children's traditions, especially those with subversive content. Mary and Herbert Knapp aptly chose the title of their 1976 classic *One Potato, Two Potato: The Secret Education of American Children.* Collecting and sharing the products of this "secret education" helps adults understand how much children learn from each other.

Children's folklore has enriched public folklore: programs that represent the depth and diversity of folk tradition. Richard Bauman foresaw this development in 1982 when he wrote that "children's folklore, representing what might aptly be called the indigenous art forms of childhood, unquestionably valued and enjoyed by the children themselves, might constitute a significant resource in the development of culturally responsive, locally relevant arts programs in the schools, together with—perhaps as an antecedent point of departure for—the general run of arts curricula that are oriented more to the fine art forms of western culture" (184). Public folklorists have used children's traditions as sources for programs at schools and festivals. The American Folklife Center at the Library of Congress offers on its Web site a "Teacher's Guide to Folklife Resources" that lists books on children's folklore. Educators with an interest in children's songs can visit the Library of Congress's Web site "See, Hear, and Sing Children's Songs," which includes audio clips, song lyrics, and photographs of children singing. Other Web sites of educational value are listed in the "Web Resources" section of this book.

In schools, presentations of children's songs, games, and other traditions have combined education with entertainment. Folklorist Kelly Armor, for example, has collected songs of inner-city children in Erie, Pennsylvania, producing the CD *Folk Songs of Champions.* Folksinger and educator Dave Ruch has used such resources to teach songs to many groups of children. This kind of educational performance replicates, to some extent, traditional instruction in singing. Since relatively large groups of children learn the songs, the likelihood of the songs' continuance in folk tradition increases.

Some children's folklore demonstrations have reminded children and teachers how much young people have in common with each other. Simon Lichman's essay "From Hopscotch to *Siji:* Generations at Play in a Cross-Cultural Setting" (2001) describes a folklore project in Israel that "addresses a number of issues that face many societies today: cultural and religious pluralism; transmission of home culture between generations; and coexistence between neighbouring but different communities" (152). Facilitators of this project, titled "Traditional Creativity through the Schools," teach Jewish and Arab children about each others' traditions, as well as the traditions of their own families. Over a two- or three-year period, children form positive relationships with other participants in the program. During the first year, children interview their own parents and grandparents to find out which games they played when they were young. With these games in mind, the children help to design a joint activity day for both Jewish and Arab children, which may include such games as Hopscotch, Chinese Jump Rope, Marbles, and Football. Older adults also participate in the joint activities. In small groups that include children of both Jewish and Arab heritage, appreciation of each others' traditions grows. Lichman explains that "the playground becomes a symbol of a world in which different cultures and generations can be together in a dynamic atmosphere of creativity, mutual interest and national coexistence" (165).

National, regional, and local folk festivals have featured children's folklore. The Smithsonian Institution's Folklife Festival in Washington, D.C., has included memorable exhibitions, such as a Double Dutch jump-rope performance in 1988 and a Stickball and Stoopball game demonstration in 2001. During the Stickball and Stoopball game exhibition, presenters combined instruction with

Girl plays in a box on a New York City street in the late 1970s. Photograph by Martha Cooper.

"constant narration and neighborhood stories" (Cohen-Stratyner 36). Festivals for local and regional audiences have also included demonstrations of children's game traditions. At the annual Battle of Plattsburgh Celebration in New York, for example, presenters have commemorated the 1814 battle by teaching children games of the early 1800s: hoop races, potato races, Rock Tag, Shadow Tag, Beanbag Toss, Horseshoes, and Gee-haw Whammy-diddle, among others. Children in the Plattsburgh area have enthusiastically learned to play these "old-time games," and some children have volunteered to help with subsequent celebrations (Ransom 29–35).

Evidence of children's folklore's impact on education also appears on Internet blogs (record-keeping Web sites). In 2006, Julia Alvarez, novelist and honorary chairman of the DREAM Project sponsored by the University of Illinois Laboratory High School, posted a handclapping rhyme on the organization's Web site. Having heard two six-year-old girls clapping and singing this rhyme in the mountains of the Dominican Republic, Alvarez realized that the girls needed better education. The rhyme follows:

Mariquita, Mariquita Mariquita, you abuser, The man I like, I'll steal him from his wife. I'll steal him, I'll steal him, I'll steal him, that's the truth, and then she'll have to be my servant and my cook. I was born at one o'clock, at two they baptized me, at three I learned of love, at four they married me, at five I had a child, by six that child was dead, we buried him at seven, I got divorced at eight, at nine I had cancer, the operation was at ten, at eleven final prayers, at twelve o'clock, the end. When my husband gets home I don't know what I'll say, you better take your shoes off and wash off your dirty smell.

Thinking about the limited opportunities for women that this rhyme reflected, Alvarez helped to found a school at Alta Gracia, a sustainable farm. The story of this realization, including the rhyme's text, has inspired high school students and adult staff members of the DREAM Project, who spend their summers volunteering and learning in the Dominican Republic.

Besides motivating adults to work with children, young people's traditions have provided a pattern for corporate executives' training. Among the "low ropes" (team-building) exercises included in executives' retreats are Moon Ball, Blind Line Up, Pass the Loop, Double Dutch, Tail Tag, and Elbow Tag. One especially intriguing exercise that mirrors children's folklore of the supernatural is Light As a Feather, also known as Helium Pole. Each participant holds one finger under a long, light pole, and the group tries to lower the pole—but it mysteriously rises! Through folk traditions kept in circulation by children, executives learn how to rely on each other and enjoy friendly competition ("Basics Kit").

How will children's folklore influence people in the future, inside and outside of the childhood underground? No matter what interactions develop, it seems clear that children's folklore will remain diverse and vigorous. In their conclusion to *Children's Folklore: A Source Book,* Felicia R. McMahon and Brian Sutton-Smith observe that we live "in a world of multiple childhoods and multiple ways in which these can be studied" (308). Remembering how much cultures, lifestyles, and viewpoints differ from each other, we can maintain a balanced outlook while delving into the wealth of details that make children's folklore such a fascinating field of study.

WORKS CITED

Alston, Philip, Stephen Parker, and John Seymour. *Children, Rights, and the Law.* Oxford: Clarendon, 1992.

Alvarez, Julia. "Letter from Honorary Chair." *Dominican Republic.* June 23, 2007. http://www.uni.uiuc.edu/gargoyle/dominican%20republic/2007/06/epiphany.html.

Armor, Kelly. "Folk Songs of Champions." Compact disc. Erie, PA: Erie Art Museum, 2004.

"Basics Kit." *The Wilderdom Store.* 2005. http://wilderdom.com/store/index.php?main_page=product_info&products_id=36.

Bauman, Richard. "Ethnography of Children's Folklore." *Children In and Out of School: Ethnography and Education.* Ed. Perry Gilmore and Allan A. Glatthorn. Washington, DC: Center for Applied Linguistics. 172–86.

Bell, L. Michael. "Cokelore." *Readings in American Folklore.* Ed. Jan Harold Brunvand. New York: Norton, 1979. 99–105.

Blank, Trevor J. "From Pop Rocks to Mentos: The Transition of Cokelore from Oral to Electronic Transmission." Paper presented at the annual Meeting of the American Folklore Society, Quebec, 2007.

Bronner, Simon J. *American Children's Folklore.* Little Rock: August, 1988.

———. "Expressing and Creating Ourselves in Childhood: A Commentary." *Children's Folklore Review* 15.1 (1992): 47–59.

———. *Folklife Studies from the Gilded Age: Object, Rite, and Custom in Victorian America.* Ann Arbor: UMI Research Press, 1987.

Buchanan, Andrea J., and Miriam Peskowitz. *The Daring Book for Girls.* New York: Harper Collins, 2007.

Carpenter, Carole H. "'Our Dreams in Action': Spirituality and Children's Play Today." *Play Today in the Primary School Playground.* Ed. Julia C. Bishop and Mavis Curtis. Buckingham, Eng., and Philadelphia: Open UP, 2001. 167–79.

Chamberlain, Alexander. *The Child and Childhood in Folk-Thought.* New York: Macmillan, 1896.

Cohen-Stratyner, Barbara. "Voices of Others: Personal Narratives in the Folklife Festival." *Voices: The Journal of New York Folklore* 33.1–2 (2007): 32–39.

Douglas, Norman. *London Street Games.* 1916. London: Chatto and Windus, 1931. Detroit: Singing Tree, 1968.

Fine, Gary Alan. "Children and Their Culture: Exploring Newell's Paradox." *Western Folklore* 39 (1980): 170–83.

———. "Folklore Diffusion through Interactive Social Networks: Conduits in a Preadolescent Community." *New York Folklore* 5.1–2 (1979): 87–126.

———. "Methodological Problems of Collecting Folklore from Children." *Children's Folklore: A Source Book*. Ed. Brian Sutton-Smith, Jay Mechling, Thomas W. Johnson, and Felicia R. McMahon. New York: Garland, 1995. 121–40.

Friedman, Thomas L. *The World Is Flat: A Brief History of the Twenty-First Century*. New York: Farrar, 2005.

Georges, Robert A., and Michael Owen Jones. *People Studying People: The Human Element in Fieldwork*. Berkeley: U of California P, 1980.

Goldstein, Kenneth S. *A Guide for Field Workers in Folklore*. Hatboro, PA: Folklore Associates, 1964.

Green, Joanne, and J.D.A. Widdowson, *Traditional English Language Genres: Continuity and Change, 1950–2000*. Sheffield: National Centre for English Cultural Tradition, 2003.

Howard, Dorothy. "Post Script, 1990" to "Folk Jingles of American Children: A Collection and Study of Rhymes Used by Children Today." Quoted in June Factor, "A Forgotten Pioneer." *Child's Play: Dorothy Howard and the Folklore of Australian Children*. Ed. Kate Darian-Smith and June Factor. Melbourne: Museum Victoria, 2005. 1–18.

"Human Subjects Position Statement." *American Folklore Society*. http://www.afsnet.org/aboutAFS/humansubjects.cfm/ethics.cfm.

Iggulden, Conn, and Hal Iggulden. *The Dangerous Book for Boys*. New York: Harper Collins, 2007.

Jackson, Bruce. *Fieldwork*. Urbana: U of Illinois P, 1987.

Kalliala, Marjatta. *Play Culture in a Changing World*. Berkshire, Eng.: Open UP, 2006.

Knapp, Mary, and Herbert Knapp. *One Potato, Two Potato: The Secret Education of American Children*. New York: Norton, 1976.

Kurmay, F. Paul. "Do Children Need a Bill of Rights? Children As More than Objects of the Law." *Connecticut Probate Law Journal* 10.2 (Spring 1996): 237–67.

Latham, Robert, and William Matthews, eds. *The Diary of Samuel Pepys*. Vol. 6. Berkeley and Los Angeles: U of California P, 1972.

Lichman, Simon. "From Hopscotch to *Siji*: Generations at Play in a Cross-Cultural Setting." *Play Today in the Primary School Playground*. Ed. Julia C. Bishop and Mavis Curtis. Buckingham, Eng., and Philadelphia: Open UP, 2001. 152–66.

Lioubart, Margarita. "New Topics and Characters of Children's Games in Today's Russia." Paper presented at the Urban Childhood Conference, Trondheim, Norway, 1997.

McMahon, Felicia R. *Not Just Child's Play: Emerging Tradition and the Lost Boys of Sudan*. Jackson: UP of Mississippi, 2007.

McMahon, Felicia R., and Brian Sutton-Smith. "The Past in the Present: Theoretical Directions for Children's Folklore." *Children's Folklore: A Source Book*. Ed. Brian Sutton-Smith, Jay Mechling, Thomas W. Johnson, and Felicia R. McMahon. New York: Garland, 1995. 293–308.

Newell, William Wells. *Games and Songs of American Children*. 1883. New York: Dover, 1963.

Norton, Edward. *Play Streets*. New York: Barnes, 1937.

Opie, Iona, and Peter Opie. *Children's Games in Street and Playground*. Oxford: Oxford UP, 1969.

———. *The Lore and Language of Schoolchildren*. Oxford: Oxford UP, 1959.

———. *Oxford Dictionary of Nursery Rhymes*. 1951. Oxford: Clarendon, 1973.

Ransom, Stanley. "Games Children Play(ed)." *Voices: The Journal of New York Folklore* 30.1–2 (2004): 29–35.

Santino, Jack. *Halloween and Other Festivals of Death and Life*. Knoxville: U of Tennessee P, 1994.

"See, Hear, and Sing Children's Songs." *America's Story from America's Library*. http://www.americaslibrary.gov/cgi-bin/page.cgi/sh/kidsongs.

Sherman, Josepha, and T.K.F. Weisskopf. *Greasy Grimy Gopher Guts: The Subversive Folklore of Childhood*. Little Rock: August, 1995.

Sobel, David. "Take Back the Afternoon: Preserving the Landscape of Childhood in Spite of Computers." *New Horizons for Learning*. June 2004. http://www.newhorizons.org/strategies/technology/sobel.htm.

Sutton-Smith, Brian. *The Ambiguity of Play*. Cambridge: Harvard UP, 1998.

———. *The Folkgames of Children*. Austin: U of Texas P, 1972.

———. *The Folkstories of Children*. Philadelphia: U of Pennsylvania P, 1981.

———. "Psychology of Children: The Triviality Barrier." *Western Folklore* 29 (1970): 1–8.

———. *Toys As Culture*. New York: Gardner, 1986.

Sutton-Smith, Brian, Jay Mechling, Thomas W. Johnson, and Felicia R. McMahon, eds. *Children's Folklore: A Source Book*. New York: Garland, 1995.

"Teacher's Guide to Folklife Resources." *American Folklife Center*. http://www.loc.gov/folklife/teachers.html.

Teitelbaum, Lee E. "Children's Rights and the Problem of Equal Respect." *Hofstra Law Review* 27.4 (Summer 1999): 799–824.

Williams, Timothy, and Cassi Feldman. "Anyone Up for Stickball? In a Play Station World, Maybe Not." *New York Times*. July 1, 2007. M25.

Wordsworth, William. "My Heart Leaps Up When I Behold." 1875. *Bartleby.com*. 2007. http://www.bartleby.com/106/286/html.

Two

Definitions and Classifications

CHILDHOOD

Since the publication of Philippe Ariès's *Centuries of Childhood* in 1962, scholars have debated the relationship between childhood and culture. Ariès's influential study traces concepts of childhood from ancient times to the twentieth century through close examination of works of art. Noting that medieval art up to the twelfth century "did not know childhood or did not attempt to portray it," Ariès identifies the seventeenth century as the time when portraits of children without adults became common (33, 46). These representations, he argues, show that a distinctive culture of childhood began in the seventeenth century. Objections to Ariès's approach have included June Factor's assertion that childhood is not an "adult-created social category"; misreading historical evidence and overlooking children's traditions has caused people to view childhood as a creation of adults. This viewpoint, Factor suggests, constitutes one of the myths about children's folklore that we need to dispel ("Three Myths" 31–33).

Concepts of childhood vary from one culture to another. American educators define as "schoolchildren" all young people from kindergarten through 12th grade, although they recognize children's ascending levels of maturity as they move through middle school and high school. In some cultures and religions, ceremonies followed by celebrations mark children's progress from childhood to maturity. Jewish boys' bar mitzvahs at age 13 and girls' bat mitzvahs at age 12, Hispanic girls' *quinceañeras* at age 15, American girls' "sweet 16" birthday parties, and North and West African boys' circumcision and girls' excision ceremonies at the onset of puberty are among the best-known passages of this kind.

Folklorists view adolescence, which begins at puberty, as an age stage that differs significantly from earlier childhood. Sue Samuelson makes a compelling case for the recognition of adolescence as a time when young people form strong relationships with peer-group members, apart from the domain of family life; these connections result in certain kinds of folklore. During the years preceding adolescence, often called preadolescence, children actively participate in peer-group activities and test boundaries established by adults.

FOLKLORE

Folklore involves communication of games, songs, stories, rituals, taunts, and other traditional content from one individual to another and from one generation to the next. In 1846, William J. Thoms introduced the term *folklore* in England. Folklorists in the 1880s and 1890s viewed folklore as survivals of an earlier, simpler way of life; now folklorists understand that all people participate in folk culture. Barre Toelken, author of *The Dynamics of Folklore*, states, "All folklore participates in a distinctive, dynamic process" (10). Variability distinguishes folklore from academic learning; textbooks stay the same (except when their authors prepare new editions), but no one tells a story or describes a game exactly the same as someone else does. Reflecting the society in which it circulates, folklore expresses people's interests, needs, and values.

Folk groups—gatherings of two or more individuals—facilitate the transmission of folklore. Age, religion, ethnicity, occupation, and interests draw people together in groups. Children constitute a distinctive age group that shares many traditions. Since the 1880s, people have recognized children's folklore as an important field of study.

PLAY

Study of play began in the late nineteenth century. G. Stanley Hall, a psychologist, was one of a number of scholars who believed that play reflected adults' activities of earlier eras. Hall's recapitulation theory suggests that children's play offers an important guide to the past. This evolutionary approach to understanding children's behavior shaped the analysis of such early collectors of childlore as Lady Alice Bertha Gomme, who interpreted the game London Bridge as an enactment of early sacrificial rites (2: 347).

In 1938, the Dutch historian Johan Huizinga published his important study *Homo Ludens* [Playing Man], which identifies play as a key component of culture. According to Huizinga, "play is a voluntary activity or occupation executed within certain fixed limits of time and place, according to rules freely accepted but absolutely binding, having its aim in itself and accompanied by a feeling of tension, joy and the consciousness that it is 'different' from 'ordinary life'" (28). Since Huizinga identified the human species as *Homo ludens,* folklore scholars have used the word *ludic* to denote playful activity.

Another significant study by the French scholar Roger Caillois, *Man, Play, and Games* (1961), suggests that play is essentially free, separate, uncertain, unproductive, rule-bound, and make-believe (9–10). Caillois divides games into four main categories: *agon* (competition), *alea* (chance), *mimicry* (simulation), and *ilinx* (vertigo). He emphasizes the importance of *paidia* (joyful improvisation), which motivates children to do new and exciting things. Caillois's concepts and terms have suggested productive directions for children's folklore scholarship. The Finnish scholar Marjatta Kalliala, for example, devotes a chapter of *Play Culture in a Changing World* (2006) to play that fits the ilinx category (94–105).

During the twentieth century, play studies became interdisciplinary and multicultural, with psychologists and anthropologists taking leadership. Jean Piaget's *Play, Dreams, and Imitation in Childhood* (1972) introduced stages of play behavior, from early childhood through the age of 12. The Anthropological Association for the Study of Play (TAASP) began in the early 1970s under the leadership of Alyce Cheska and Brian Sutton-Smith.

Helen B. Schwartzman's *Transformations: The Anthropology of Children's Play* (1978) offers representative ethnographic reports from Asia, Oceania, the Americas, Africa, the Near East, and Europe. Schwartzman covers the main areas of play study through the late 1970s, including evolutionary and developmental studies, diffusionism, functional analysis, studies of culture and personality, communication studies, structural and cognition studies, ecology, and ethology (study of animal behavior).

Recent play studies have reflected openness to new approaches, as well as multiculturalism and globalization. In *The Future of Play Theory* (1995), edited by Anthony D. Pellegrini, scholars consider play as progress, power, and fantasy; this collection of essays honors Brian Sutton-Smith's accomplishments as a leading scholar of play. Another significant study, *Play and Intervention* (1994), edited by Joop Hellendoorn, Rimmert van der Kooij, and Brian Sutton-Smith, explores how play therapy helps children with various needs. *Play Today in the Primary School Playground* (2001), edited by Julia C. Bishop and Mavis Curtis, examines play among children of different nationalities and ethnicities; it also classifies play traditions by verbal, imaginative, and physical content (14). Kalliala's *Play Culture in a Changing World* (2006) succinctly reviews past play scholarship, presents examples of Finnish children's play, and advocates the creation of a rich play environment for children (139).

Speech Play

Speech play demonstrates children's joy in manipulating language. While riddles, jokes, rhymes, and songs all involve speech play, folklorists tend to classify those forms of children's folklore as separate genres and to consider shorter utterances, such as slang terms, tongue twisters, and sentences from secret languages, as part of the broader genre of speech play. Two excellent surveys of children's speech play are "Children's Traditional Speech Play and Child Language" by Barbara Kirshenblatt-Gimblett and Mary Sanches (1976) and "Rhythm, Repetition and Rhetoric" by J.D.A. Widdowson (2001).

Folklorists, linguists, and other scholars have traced the development of children's slang, admiring its creativity. Norman Douglas's *London Street Games* offers diverse terms for games and toys; large marbles, for example, were called *bonsers, bonks, bucks,* or *bonsters* before 1931 (69). One English slang term, *cool,* has continued to mean "good" since the Beatnik movement of the 1950s. During the 1990s and the early twenty-first century, *wicked good, phat,* and *sick* were terms of high praise. The *Berkeley High School Slang Dictionary,* assembled by students in 2004, includes a plethora of terms for "friend," including *homey, dude, cousin, bro, nizzel,* and *blood.* There are also many names for marijuana, including *endoe, chronic, dojah, blunt, joint, pinner, pookie, bud,* and *bammer.* Terms for illegal drugs change frequently, since kids hope to avoid parents' and teachers' notice. June Factor's *Kidspeak: A Dictionary of Australian Children's Words, Expressions and Games* (2000) similarly surveys the folk speech of children in Australia.

Tongue twisters challenge children to repeat difficult sequences of sounds. Popular English tongue twisters include "Peter Piper picked a peck of pickled peppers," "She sells seashells by the seashore," and "How much wood would a woodchuck chuck if a woodchuck could chuck wood?" Some tongue twisters threaten to embarrass the speaker. It is hard to recite the following rhyme without saying a forbidden word: "I slit a sheet; a sheet I slit. Upon the slitted sheet I sit" (Opie and Opie, *I Saw Esau* 63). With a tongue twister like this one, saying the wrong word can give more pleasure to other children than saying the right one.

French children have practiced repeating "Si six scies scient six cigares, six cent scies scient six cent cigares" [If six sawyers saw six cigars, six hundred sawyers saw six hundred cigars]. For German children, the tongue twister *(Zungenbrecher)* "Bierbrauer Bauer braut braunes Bier" [Beer brewer Bauer brews brown beer] has offered an interesting challenge. Such tongue twisters exist around the world.

Another demonstration of linguistic skill is the spoonerism, which got its name from Oxford professor William Archibald Spooner (1844–1930). Switching consonants or syllables of adjacent words with each other, children recite a rhyme or verse that sounds like nonsense. One example of this genre, popular from the late nineteenth century to the 1970s, is "Mardon me, padam, this pie is occupewed. May I sew you to a sheet in another chart of the perch?" [Pardon me, madam, this pew is occupied. May I show you to a seat in another part of the church?] Other sayings attributed to Spooner include "The Lord is a shoving leopard" and "It is kisstomary to cuss the bride."

Secret languages give children the pleasure of confusing their parents and teachers. Since children usually have to figure out the language of adults, it is fun for children to make adults struggle to understand their languages. William Wells Newell's detailed description of late nineteenth-century children's secret languages in *Games and Songs of American Children* shows that some patterns of secret-language development have remained relatively similar. Newell explains that Hog Latin involves "the addition of the syllable *ery*, preceded by the sound of hard *g*, to every word." In Hog Latin, the question "Will you go with me?" becomes "Wiggery youggery goggery wiggery miggery?" (24). The term *Pig Latin* also arose in the nineteenth century. Speakers of Pig Latin in the United States move the first consonant or consonant cluster to the end of words and add *ay*. Children in eastern Finland enjoy using a syllable-switching language called pig's German (Virtanen 34). Closer in form to the Hog Latin language that Newell encountered is Op Talk, which involves adding *op* to each consonant or consonant cluster.

In the 1990s, American teenagers started to use the Izzle language, sometimes called Snoop Speak because of its attribution to the rap singer Snoop Doggy Dogg. Speakers of this language add the suffix *izzle* to a word's initial consonant or consonant cluster. *Sure* becomes *shizzle, scrabble* becomes *scrizzle,* and so on.

Twenty-first-century children in the United States and other nations use letter codes to communicate with each other on computers and cellular phones. Many e-mails, instant messages (IMs), and mobile text messages include such acronyms as LOL (laugh out loud), G2G (got to go), and LMIRL (let's meet in real life). MOS (Mom over shoulder), PAW (parents are watching), and CD9 (code 9) warn friends to respond in acronyms that hovering parents will find difficult to understand.

Because Web sites like Teenchatdecoder.com help parents understand their children's letter codes, kids continually develop new codes; for example, CD8 (code 8) may replace the better-known CD9. Stefanie Olsen notes that the addition of nonsense words such as *ittica* between acronyms also makes it harder for parents to read what their children have written. Coming up with new terms gives children the dual pleasure of creating linguistic variations and one-upping their parents.

Some text-messaging codes are gender-specific. In Japan, for example, teenage girls' texting, known as Gal Go, creatively combines Japanese characters. Gal Go is a specialized form of *ko-gyaru-go,* "high school girl talk," which developed in Japan in the late 1990s.

RIDDLES, JOKES, AND ROUTINES OF VICTIMIZATION

Riddles

In *Children's Riddling* (1979), John H. McDowell defines the riddle as "an interrogative ludic routine incorporating some form of contrived ambiguity" (88). Interrogative routines involve dynamics of power. McDowell explains that the riddler (the asker of the riddle) has "final authority on the correct solution" but "may not disavow a correct solution" (132). The riddle "What's black and white and red all over?" has drawn such diverse responses as "a newspaper," "an embarrassed zebra," and "a bleeding nun." If the riddler wants to give the riddlee a hard time, he or she can keep the session going until the desired answer emerges.

While many question/answer sequences qualify as riddles, those that emphasize humor more than the guessing process can be called *riddle-jokes*. Folklorists' terms for these expressive forms vary. Simon J. Bronner's *American Children's Folklore* distinguishes riddles from riddle parodies, which mock established riddles; riddling questions, which ask the riddlee to identify a referent; and joking questions, which emphasize humorous punch lines (114–18). Danielle Roemer's 1995 study covers both verbal and nonverbal riddles.

Some riddles are easier to remember because of their rhymes. Iona and Peter Opie include some fine examples of rhyming riddles in their *Lore and Language of Schoolchildren;* one of these, from a 13-year-old girl, is "White and thin, red within, with a nail on the end" (77). Its answer: "A finger." Rhyming riddles have circulated in oral tradition for centuries, but nonrhyming questions have been more popular in recent years.

The oldest known riddle takes the form of a three-part question. The Opies present a variant of the ancient Greek "Sphinx riddle" from a 15-year-old girl: "What walks on four feet in the morning, two feet at noon, and three feet in the evening?" (76). The answer: "A man." An alternative answer, more suitable for the early twenty-first century, would be "a person."

Young children who have not yet mastered the complexity of the riddle may describe a referent without trying to confuse the listener. Brian Sutton-Smith calls such questions "pre-riddles" ("Developmental Structural Account" 114–15); McDowell calls them "descriptive routines." Among the descriptive routines in McDowell's data sample are "What's red? *A rose*," "What has three wheels and pedals? *A tricycle*," and "What's brown and its round and it gots the leaves on it? *A tree*" (244).

Riddles that embarrass or surprise the riddlee are generally called *catch riddles*. One such riddle that circulated while I was in high school was "What do virgins eat for breakfast?" If the riddlee said nothing, the riddler could assume that the riddlee was not a virgin. My friends and I learned to avoid being caught by saying "toast," "eggs," or the name of any other breakfast food.

Closely related to the riddle is the puzzle, which provides enough details so that the listener can come up with a solution. According to Sarah Lash, the teller of a situational puzzle describes a situation, then asks the audience to explain how the situation occurred. Some puzzles seem solvable but are actually catches. When asked "If a plane crashes on the border between Kansas and Colorado, in which state would you bury the survivors?" you might spend some time figuring out which state seems most appropriate; however, survivors do not want to be buried alive.

Jokes

Like riddles, jokes use verbal trickery to amuse and impress listeners. Some children's jokes, such as knock-knock routines, follow a well-established question-and-answer format, but others tell detailed stories. Folklorists call jokes that go on for quite a while and culminate in a tricky or ridiculous punch line *shaggy dog stories;* other kinds of jokes include dirty jokes, sick or tasteless jokes, ethnic jokes, and numskull jokes. Following cycles of interest to youngsters, jokes flourish, then fade; sometimes, dormant jokes become popular again later on.

Since the publication of Sigmund Freud's *Jokes and Their Relation to the Unconscious* (1905), scholars have analyzed the significance of dirty jokes. Gershon Legman states, "The smutty joke is like a denudation of a person of the opposite sex toward whom the joke is directed. Through the utterance of obscene words, the person attacked is forced to picture the parts of the body in question, or the sexual act, and is shown that the aggressor himself pictures the same thing" (12). While this Freudian definition focuses on sexual and hostile elements that deserve attention, it presumes that dirty jokes are mainly told by males to females (or by females to males) to make the listener feel embarrassed and uncomfortable. Many dirty jokes told by children do not follow such a pattern. More commonly, children share what they know about sex through telling dirty jokes, enjoying the chance to use taboo words in stories kept secret from parents and teachers. Scholars who have analyzed dirty jokes according to Freudian theory include Martha Wolfenstein and Alan Dundes; their contributions to children's folklore scholarship are discussed in chapter 4.

Sick or tasteless jokes introduce subjects in such bad taste that they provoke nervous laughter. Following current concerns and crises, sick and tasteless joke cycles rise and fall. Although their tastelessness horrifies some people, these jokes serve the purpose of releasing tension related to difficult subjects. Tasteless jokes about disabled individuals express people's worry about disabilities. A case in point is the Helen Keller riddle-joke cycle, an example of which is "How did Helen Keller's parents punish her? They rearranged the furniture." Some tasteless joke cycles are related to specific historical crises. When the AIDS epidemic became a frightening subject in Europe and the United States in the early 1980s, both children and adults began to tell AIDS jokes. The explosion of the American space shuttle *Challenger* in 1986 gave rise to such riddle-jokes as "What does NASA stand for? Need Another Seven Astronauts" (Simons 263). Other tasteless riddle-jokes have sprung up after the deaths of celebrities, including England's Princess Diana ("What does DIANA stand for? Died in a nasty accident"). Through such jokes, children and adults have released tension by laughing at subjects that have no intrinsic humorous value.

Similar in their level of social inappropriateness, ethnic jokes push the envelope of acceptability by disadvantageously comparing one ethnic group with another. Such jokes tend to criticize relatively recent immigrants and people of neighboring countries. In Norway, for example, people tell Swedish jokes; residents of Sweden tell jokes about Norwegians. American ethnic jokes have tended to characterize the targeted ethnic group as having little money, poor hygiene, and low motivation to succeed. Just as tasteless jokes release tension about worrisome subjects, ethnic jokes call for laughter about interethnic tension.

Less injurious but still offensive to some people are numskull jokes, which make fun of stupidity. In the 1950s and 1960s, "little moron" riddle-jokes flourished ("Why did the little moron throw his clock out the window? Because he wanted to see time fly"). Blonde jokes have been popular in the 1990s and early twenty-first century. In her essay "Dumb Blondes, Dan Quayle, and Hillary Clinton: Gender, Sexuality, and Stupidity in Jokes" (1997), Jeannie B. Thomas suggests that "the contemporary rise of dumb-blonde jokes may be linked to the rise in women's visibility in public places and in places of power since the women's movement of the 1960s and 1970s" (278). One of the riddle-jokes in her article, collected from a 13-year-old boy, is "Why does the blonde climb over the glass wall? To see what's on the other side" (281). Thomas aptly notes the connection between this joke's glass wall and the glass ceiling that has made it difficult for women to seek higher-level employment (309).

Routines of Victimization

In routines of victimization, one child embarrasses or shocks the other by making him or her do something that ends badly. John H. McDowell explains that routines of victimization "countenance such infractions as lying without compunction, breaking frames without warning, openly contradicting self and other, making unsavory allegations concerning other, and in some cases actually punishing other with physical violence" (39). Catch riddles belong to this broader category, which includes both verbal and partly verbal interactions. Mary and Herbert Knapp call routines of this kind "ambush games" (76–77); the Opies call them "tricks" and "traps" (*Lore and Language* 57–72), and Leea Virtanen calls them "traps," citing several examples (54).

RHYMES

Counting-Out Rhymes

Counting-out rhymes give children formulae for choosing players or designating someone to take the role of "it." H. C. Bolton's *The Counting-Out Rhymes of Children* (1888) was the first study of such rhymes. Bolton states that people used counting-out rhymes for divination, establishing patterns to identify sacrificial victims (26). The idea that counting-out rhymes originated in ancient Druids' sacrifices has appealed to many people. Elliott Oring's essay "On the Tradition and Mathematics of Counting-Out" (1997) refutes Bolton's premise, suggesting that stories about mathematical formulas for choosing victims have a better basis in fact. The "Josephus problem," for example, concerns legends about Jewish soldiers' determination of who will commit suicide while trapped in a cave by Roman soldiers during the Jewish-Roman War of the first century A.D. Flavius Josephus carefully chooses his place in the circle of soldiers to make sure that he will survive the counting process; he is the only soldier who lives to explain what happened.

Studies of children's counting-out rhymes have shown that children know how to choose players they prefer. In Kenneth S. Goldstein's "Strategy in Counting-Out" (1971), based on fieldwork with children in Philadelphia, he identifies such forms of manipulation as "skipping over," "calculation," and "rhyme extension" (167–78). Later studies have had similar results. Andy Arleo's essay "Strategy in Counting-Out: Evidence from Saint-Nazaire, France" (1991) offers interesting examples. Sitting in a circle, children wait for the counter to tap one foot or fist of each participant; occasionally the children stand up and wait for a tap on the chest. To get the preferred outcome, a counter skips certain players, starts with a particular player, or adds extra words. One formulaic addition is "Pouf pouf. You will be the Wolf, but as the king and the queen don't want this [to happen], it won't be you." In his survey of French children's counting-out behavior in 1981, Arleo found that 82.1 percent of the children viewed counting-out as a process of artful manipulation (26–27).

The most thorough sourcebook of counting-out rhymes is Roger Abrahams's and Lois Rankin's *Counting-Out Rhymes: A Dictionary* (1980). The second volume of Joanne Green's and J.D.A. Widdowson's *Traditional English Language Genres: Continuity and Change* (2003) offers important information about which counting-out rhymes have stood the test of time in England, with "One Potato, Two Potato" and "Ip Dip Do" at the top of the list (361).

Handclapping Rhymes

In *The Singing Game* (1985), Iona and Peter Opie explain that handclapping flourished from the end of the nineteenth century to World War I. From then until the 1950s "the art of hand-clapping did not exactly die out; but it came a poor third to ball-bouncing and skipping amongst the games of agility. It was not till the wave of sparkling and spirited chants came over from America that it would enjoy a revival" (443). Since the 1960s, handclaps have delighted children in many parts of the world. Video clips of handclapping games on YouTube in 2007 came from Australia, Guatemala, Nepal, Kenya, Japan, and the United Kingdom, among other countries.

In the 1960s, African American girls' handclapping games attracted scholars' attention. The film *Pizza Pizza Daddy-O* by Bess Lomax Hawes shows African American girls doing handclaps on a Los Angeles playground in 1967. Kyra D. Gaunt's in-depth study *The Games Black Girls Play* (2006) presents girls' clapping games as fluid combinations of sound, sense, and motion. Gaunt states, "The kinetic orality of African American musical aesthetics that girls learn to inhabit through these games points to a lived phenomenology of a gendered blackness" (57). Among the important points that Gaunt makes are relationships between clapping games and hip-hop music. The game Down Down Baby, for example, has a connection to the songs "Country Grammar" by the hip-hop singer Nelly (2000) and "Shimmy Shimmy Ko Ko Pop" by Little Anthony and the Imperials (1956), as well as a movement in the song "Ballin' the Jack" (1913). These connections, Gaunt suggests, make it possible "to consider that women and girls are playing a vital role in the production of popular taste" (101–2).

Jump-Rope Rhymes

Jumping or skipping rope has entertained children since the Middle Ages. Norman Douglas notes in *London Street Games* that boys used to participate in jumping rope before it became a game for girls. Douglas mentions the popularity of rhymes for choosing a sweetheart's name, such as "Black-currant—red currant—raspberry tart: tell me the name of your sweetheart" (27). The jumper recites letters of the alphabet; if she misses on "D," that will be the initial of her sweetheart's first name. This divinatory function of jump-rope rhymes has continued into the twenty-first century, although the rhymes have changed to some extent.

Roger Abrahams's *Jump-Rope Rhymes: A Dictionary* (1969) offers an excellent list of jump-rope rhymes with bibliographic citations. His study and others focus more on the rhymes than the actions that accompany them, but recent approaches have changed. In her 1995 essay "Double Dutch and Double Cameras," Ann Richman Beresin observes, "the privileging of game texts by collectors of children's folklore has been directly related to the available methodologies for folk-game study" (75). Her own analysis of working-class girls' Double Dutch (two-rope) performances involved the use of two video cameras: one in a second-floor window and another down in the schoolyard where the children played.

Girl jumps rope in New York City in the late 1970s.
Photograph by Martha Cooper.

This approach effectively captures the movements and context of jump rope, as
well as verbal interaction.

Autograph Rhymes   yearbook

Children began to write verses in each others' autograph albums in the late
1800s. Closely related to verses on Valentine's Day and other seasonal cards, early
autograph rhymes expressed the importance of friendship. In his study of nineteenth-century autograph books in New York, W. K. McNeil notes the popularity of rhymes about friendship and memory; he also notes the popularity of letter
codes such as "YYUR, YYUB, ICUR YY4me" [Too wise you are, too wise you be,
I see you are too wise for me].

Simon J. Bronner's *American Children's Folklore* offers a representative selection of twentieth-century children's autograph rhymes, including many funny
and critical verses (83–95). Some rhymes comment humorously on courtship,

marriage, and children, all of which represent the mysterious future. Expectations of continuing friendship emerge in rhymes such as "When you get older and have twins, call on me for safety pins."

Although autograph albums have become less common than they used to be, students still write in each other's yearbooks and sign T-shirts, casts on broken limbs, and other objects. Elementary-school children enjoy reading books like Joanna Cole's *Yours Till Banana Splits: 201 Autograph Rhymes* (1995), which help to keep the old rhyming traditions alive.

TAUNTS AND COUNTERTAUNTS

The *Oxford English Dictionary* confirms the longevity of children's taunts, which some folklorists call *jeers*. *Greedy-gut(s)* appeared in print in 1550, *fatty* in 1797, *cry-baby* in 1852, and *tattle-tale* in 1889. Iona and Peter Opie identify taunts for children who behave in certain ways: *spoilsports, sourpusses, fools, copycats, cowards, crybabies, sneaks, bullies,* and others (*Lore and Language* 186–88). Such taunts correct what children perceive as inappropriate behavior. Mary and Herbert Knapp offer examples of rhyming taunts related to children's last names, such as "Gold, Gold, you eat mold" and "Brown, Brown, you're a clown" (63).

In the second half of the twentieth century, some of the most common taunts of English-speaking children were "Liar, liar, pants on fire," "Baby, baby, stick your head in gravy," "Pink, pink, you stink," and various insults from the African American "dozens" tradition, such as "Your mama's a doorknob" (Bronner 40–42). To ward off an insult, a child might use the countertaunt "I'm rubber, you're glue, everything you say bounces back to you" or "I know you are, but what am I?" The Knapps provide a good selection of countertaunts in *One Potato, Two Potato* (68–69).

In 2003 a study at the University of Central Lancashire in England showed that more than a third of primary-school children with cellular phones had received name-calling text messages. Some of these messages sounded threatening enough to qualify as bullying, according to Sean Coughlan. Although such information is not available for all schools, it seems clear that name-calling through text messaging has entered the childhood underground.

SONGS

Little children learn simple songs from their parents, preschool teachers, and other caregivers. Some songs, such as "Twinkle, Twinkle Little Star" and "Mary Had a Little Lamb," belong to the rich tradition of nursery rhymes chronicled by Iona and Peter Opie in their *Oxford Dictionary of Nursery Rhymes*. Lullabies calm children down; alphabet songs help them remember the letters of the alphabet. As they listen to such songs, children learn that singing combines entertainment with functionality.

In "Songs, Poems, and Rhymes," C. W. Sullivan III observes that children "will make up songs and rhymes about anything and everything" (159). They discard many songs soon after coming up with them; few songs last for long, but the process of invention and transmission keeps traditional material circulating (159–60). In some settings, such as bus rides on the way to summer camp, songs give youngsters a chance to have some irreverent fun.

Parodies, which subvert "serious" songs, TV commercial jingles, and other songs created by adults, have a strong appeal. Simon J. Bronner devotes one chapter of his *American Children's Folklore* to children's creative and traditional parodies (95–112). Josepha Sherman's and T.K.F. Weisskopf's *Greasy Grimy Gopher Guts* (1995) includes variants of many memorable song parodies, some of which are spectacularly gross and cleverly phrased.

In "Gopher Guts and Army Trucks" (1999), Josepha Sherman suggests that songs and rhymes reveal "children's awareness of changing cultural and societal mores" (17). Her study of songs about torturing teachers shows that imagery has become increasingly violent since the late 1960s. In the 1950s, for example, many parodies of "The Battle Hymn of the Republic" included the line "I bopped her on the bean / With a rotten tangerine"; in the mid-1990s, versions of that line included "I met her in the attic / With a loaded automatic" and "I met her at the bank / With a U.S. Army tank" (18–19). Such changes reflect a higher tolerance for graphic violence in the culture of adults, closely observed—and creatively expressed—by children.

CHEERS

First collected from African American girls in the 1970s, cheers alternate a group's words with the words of soloists. Girls chant rhymes while clapping, stamping their feet, and doing body pats. Unlike clapping games, cheers do not involve one participant touching another. In *The Games Black Girls Play*, Kyra D. Gaunt explains that a cheer, known in some cities as a *scold* or a *step,* "names individual members, while also signifying their unique group identity" (76). Gaunt's detailed discussion of certain cheers' history demonstrates the continuity and creativity of African American girls' rhyming traditions.

Azizi Powell, creator of the Web site Cocojams.com, distinguishes "foot stomping cheers" from cheerleaders' cheers at games. Foot-stomping cheers involve standing in a line and taking turns stepping forward to do a solo; cheerleaders at games do fewer solos. Powell suggests that both kinds of cheers borrow elements from each other and that foot-stomping cheers take material from black and Latina dance-style cheerleaders.

GAMES

Imaginative Games

Iona and Peter Opie explain in *Children's Games in Street and Playground* that imaginative or "pretending" games have a long history; boys took the roles of judges and magistrates in ancient Rome, and Flemish children imitated weddings, christenings, and religious processions in the sixteenth century (330–31). Although our knowledge of such games in earlier eras is limited, twentieth-century studies have proven the breadth of children's imaginative game playing. The Opies' study includes the games Mothers and Fathers, School, Road Accidents, Horses, Storybook World, War, and Cops and Robbers, as well as Fairies and Witches. It also mentions such interesting imitations of current events as the Great Train Robbery, based on a famous heist in England in 1963, and Assassination, based on the assassination of U.S. President John F. Kennedy in 1961 (330–44).

Leea Virtanen's *Children's Lore* describes a number of imaginative games played by Finnish children (31–33). In Amanda Dargan and Steven Zeitlin's *City Play* (1990), New York City children's enactment of drug dealers' routines is one of many street games. Marc Armitage's "The Ins and Outs of School Playground Play" (2001) analyzes imaginative games played in the United Kingdom (46–54). My own observations of children's games in New York in the 1990s indicate that firefighters, police, teachers, doctors, Native Americans, film and television stars, and wild animals have inspired vigorous role-playing by children of elementary-school age.

Psychologists' studies offer important insights into the patterns and meaning of children's imaginative play. Selma Fraiberg's *The Magic Years* (1959) explores children's need for imaginative activity in early childhood. One of the best studies with a bearing on children's folklore is Jerome L. Singer's *The Child's World of Make-Believe* (1973). Singer distinguishes between high-fantasy children, whose play includes many imaginative elements, and low-fantasy children, who have less interest in "let's pretend" games.

Finger Games

Very young children learn finger games such as Peek-a-boo! from their parents and other adults. Once children are old enough to go to school, they learn different finger games from friends. Some child-taught finger games simply amuse the learner, but others serve as routines of victimization.

One finger game that has traveled around the world is Rock, Paper, Scissors *(jan ken pon)*, which first became popular in nineteenth-century Japan. In this game, two fingers representing scissors beat paper (an outstretched hand), paper beats rock (a balled-up fist), and rock beats scissors. In the older Slug version *(mushi-ken)*, snake beats frog, frog beats slug, and slug beats snake ("Origins of Rock, Paper, Scissors"). Early twenty-first-century Japanese teenagers have played this game with video cameras, watching each others' gestures on their own screens. This use of technology allows children to play the game at the same time no matter how much distance separates them.

Noncompetitive finger games often accompany rhymes or brief narratives. One finger game that American children enjoyed playing in the 1950s was "here is the church (interlace fingers), here is the steeple (raise one finger). Open the doors (spread thumbs, turn hands over) and see all the people!" Some children still learn this game, but it has become less common than it once was.

Chalk Diagram Games

One of the oldest games documented by folklorists is Hopscotch or Hoppy, once played by Roman soldiers. Children usually play these games on chalk diagrams that they have drawn themselves. Alice Bertha Gomme includes 10 Hopscotch diagrams in her *Traditional Games of England, Scotland, and Ireland* (1; 224); William Wells Newell includes one of the most common diagrams in *Games and Songs of American Children.* He notes that New Yorkers call the top of the diagram "Pot"; Austrians call it "the Temple," and Italians call it "the Bell" (188). Dorothy Howard's thorough documentation of Hopscotch games in Australia has added to folklorists' understanding of how the game has developed around the world (Darian-Smith and Factor 67–85). Simon J. Bronner's *American Children's Folklore* includes an excellent set of Hopscotch diagrams (189–97).

Skelly, which originated in New York City in the first half of the twentieth century, involves shooting bottle caps, poker chips, or other objects into the center of a diagram, sometimes called the "skull." In *City Play* (1990), Amanda Dargan and Steven Zeitlin explain the dynamics of Skelly caps: "The caps, especially when weighted with tar, cork, pennies, melted crayons, orange peels, wax, or almost anything, skim nicely along concrete surfaces with the sideways flick of the finger—a well-weighted cap can be effective in knocking an opponent's caps off the board" (84). Although Skelly diagrams seldom adorn New York City's streets in the twenty-first century, they often appear at street game revivals.

Running and Chasing Games

Games that involve running and chasing fit numerous categories. Iona and Peter Opie's *Children's Games in Street and Playground* devotes separate chapters to chasing games, such as French Touch and Daddy Whacker; catching games, such as Prisoner's Base; seeking games, such as Hide-and-Seek; hunting games, such as Hare and Hounds; racing games, such as Letters and Colours; and exerting games, such as Tug of War and Red Rover. Since it is not possible to describe all of these categories in detail, the general term *running and chasing game* is used here.

Tag, usually called Tig or Tiggy in the United Kingdom and former British colonies, gives one child the role of "it" or "he." This child chases the rest of the group and eventually touches someone, at which point the newly tagged child becomes "it." Simple reversal of roles and actions makes this game easy for young children to play. Variants include Freeze Tag, Puerto-Rican Tag, Octopus Tag, and Flashlight Tag in the United States and Tunnel Tig, Aeroplane Tig, Hospital Tig, and Toilet Tig in the United Kingdom (Mansfield 25).

In the chasing game Hare and Hounds, the child designated as hare runs away to hide; all the rest of the players, called hounds, pursue the hare as quickly as they can. Alan Dundes applies structural theory to this game in his essay "On Game Morphology," which identifies an intriguing difference between game structure and folktale structure. While the folktale has a one-dimensional plot sequence, games like Hare and Hounds have a double structure with different lacks and consequences. The hare wants to go home, but if the hounds catch him, he loses the game; the hounds want to catch the hare, but if they do not catch him before he gets home, they lose the game (337–38). Even though the game has a double plot, its intrinsic similarity to the folktale's structure offers interesting possibilities for analysis.

Ball Games

Since folk ball games require very little equipment—just a ball and, in some cases, a stick or another object—they are easy to play. William Wells Newell devotes a chapter of his *Games and Songs of American Children* (1883) to ball games, including "Base-ball," "Hand-ball," "Stool-ball," and "Hat-ball" (175–93). Newell views ball games as belonging to boys, but Norman Douglas's London Street Games (1916/1931) lists many ball games played by both boys and girls: Rounders, Head Game, Daggles, and Broken Bottle, among others.

Iona and Peter Opie explain that in games such as Ball Tag or Ball He, the ball "becomes an extension of the chaser" (*Children's Games* 73). Besides making it easier to tag someone, a ball can get someone's attention quickly. William Wells Newell describes the popular game of Call-ball, in which a boy throws a ball against a house while calling out another player's name (181). This game resembles the contemporary game of Spud, in which the child whose number is called tries to hit the closest player with the ball.

Girl plays ball in Innsbruck, Austria, in the summer of
1992. Photograph by Geoffrey Gould.

For urban children, ball games on sidewalks and in vacant lots have become
cherished traditions. New York City's street game culture began in the mid-
nineteenth century, when crowded city blocks left little room for play. Two popular ball games were Stoopball, played on a building's front steps or stoop, and
Stickball, played in a street, parking lot, or schoolyard with a ball and a broom-
stick (Dargan and Zeitlin 10–86).

Changing seasons bring different kinds of ball games. Winter involves snowball games and snowball fights, while summer offers a rich variety of games with
large and small balls. Indoor ball games such as Ping-Pong become more exciting
when a balloon takes the place of the usual ping-pong ball and the rules change to
suit the players. Hockey, usually played in a rink or on a street with a ball or puck,
develops a new dimension of wonder when played indoors with frozen Cornish
hens replacing pucks. Children's creativity continually seeks exciting variants of
familiar pursuits.

Boy/Girl Games

Folklorists have studied children's and adolescents' kissing games since the
nineteenth century. Other games that focus on interaction between boys and girls
have received less attention. Because this domain includes games such as Truth

or Dare that focus on interactions other than kissing, the term *boy/girl games* is used here.

Alice Bertha Gomme's *Traditional Games of England, Scotland, and Ireland* includes examples of late nineteenth-century kissing games. In Kiss in the Ring, for example, a child walks around a ring of players. Dropping a handkerchief behind one child means that the child will get a kiss if he or she can catch the dropper of the handkerchief (1: 305–10).

Brian Sutton-Smith's "The Kissing Games of Adolescents in Ohio" (1972) offers detailed analysis of such popular games as Spin the Bottle, Post Office, Winks, Mistletoe Kissing, and Necking. Sutton-Smith explains that traditional kissing games "provide a guarantee of certain gratifications, in this case relationship with the opposite sex, but they place limitations upon excess" (489). Games such as Biting the Apple and Passing the Orange give children a chance to touch lips briefly while performing a ridiculous task. Mary and Herbert Knapp describe a variety of kissing games in *One Potato, Two Potato* (216–20). In the 1990s and early twenty-first century, a popular game played by teenagers was Pass the Card, which involves passing a card from one person's mouth to another's. For a description of this game and its variants, see chapter 3.

Dangerous Games

Dangerous games frighten parents and teachers. In worst-case scenarios, such games cause injury or death. It is important to understand the appeal of such games for young people. Dangerous games let children prove their courage and skill. Insulated by the assurance of youth, players may not hesitate to jump into a game that looks risky. Adults, having had more experience, know that tragedies can happen. Parents tell stories about tragic outcomes of games to their children; stories of this kind appear in newspapers and on the Internet. As more information circulates, the likelihood of preventing tragic deaths improves.

Iona and Peter Opie identify a broad range of "daring games" in *Children's Games in Street and Playground* (263–74). Among these games are Truth, Dare, Promise, or Opinion; Follow My Leader; and Get the Coward; all of these involve one player following another's lead or instructions to do risky things. Two road games, Last Across and Chicken, necessitate taking risks in streets: the former on foot, the latter in cars. The Opies' last subcategory for games of this kind is "Misplaced Audacity," which includes taking risks with knives, swings, and roller-towels. Although roller-towels might seem harmless, they become dangerous when twisted around a child's neck to cause loss of consciousness. Dangling Man, the Spinning Game, and Faint Game are all folk names for this kind of activity. The Opies suggest that the main cause of such game playing is "wonder and curiosity" related to inexperience rather than bravado (273–74). While this positive interpretation seems reasonable, we should also consider the impact of

Boy jumps from a fire escape onto a mattress in New York City in the late 1970s. Photograph by Martha Cooper.

peer pressure, which makes some children feel they cannot refuse to play. The pressure to play such games emerges in Gary Hall's descriptions of Chicken collected in the early 1970s in Indiana and North Carolina (74–75), as well as in Carlos Rodriguez's account of "jumping rooftops" in New York in Martha Cooper's *Street Play* (12).

PRANKS

According to Richard S. Tallman's study (1974), the prankster or practical joker strives "to fool someone, to have fun at the expense of someone else" (269). Tallman classifies pranks as benevolent, initiatory, or malevolent. Some pranks succeed, while others fail because the prankster has gotten caught, the victim has not been fooled, or the prank has backfired (262–74). Marilyn Jorgensen's "Teases and Pranks" (1995) suggests differentiation between malicious pranks and benevolent teases and tricks; pranks and tricks deceive, but teases do not (214). Pranks tend to be more extensive and premeditated than brief routines of victimization.

Elementary-school and middle-school students have played countless April Fool's Day pranks, documented by Iona and Peter Opie in *The Lore and Language of Schoolchildren* (243–47). Halloween pranks have caused much damage and illicit joy. Such pranks should be examined in the context of Halloween legends and expectations (Dégh 233–42).

Another kind of prank involves telephone calls. One of the oldest prank phone call questions, from the days when men chewed Prince Albert tobacco, is "Do you have Prince Albert in a can?" If the listener says "Yes," the caller replies, "Well then, you'd better let him out!" Twenty-first-century communication technology lets phone call recipients use caller ID, but clever prank callers can block their own numbers to protect themselves from punishment.

High school pranks follow certain well-established traditions. One of the most popular traditions involves letting animals loose in a high school's hallways. As graduation pranks during the 1990s and the early twenty-first century, high school students put numbers on pigs (one, two, three, and five, for example) before letting the pigs run free in their school. When school officials caught the pigs, they wondered whether one pig was missing.

At summer camps, campers and counselors have become skilled pranksters. I. Sheldon Posen suggests that most camp pranks fit two closely connected categories: scatological and sexual. Scatological pranks involve excrement; for example, campers may put a sleeping friend's hand in warm water, hoping that the friend will wet the bed. Examples of sexual pranks include stealing underwear and giving someone a wedgie (causing discomfort by pulling up the waistband of the person's underwear). Certain pranks have close connections to ghost stories; a ghost that a counselor has just described may appear or make frightening noises. Posen suggests that prank etiquette necessitates a proper response from the victimized individual; even if that person does not think the prank was funny, he or she must laugh (303–9). Jay Mechling explains the process of "taking a prank well" in his 2001 study *On My Honor: Boy Scouts and the Making of American Youth* (107–9).

Certain pranks cause alarm that may, in extreme cases, lead to the arrest of the pranksters. After the Columbine High School massacre on April 20, 1999, pranks involving fake guns or bombs resulted in visits from local police. The destruction of the World Trade Center in New York City on September 11, 2001, increased people's worry about possible explosives and dangerous substances such as anthrax. According to Zehr, after students played an anthrax prank at a middle school in Kentucky, the school district's risk manager said, "Any kid with a pen and some flour can bring a district to its knees." During a crisis, a prank can be reclassified from childish amusement to criminal offense.

NARRATIVES

Tales

Tales are relatively short, entertaining narratives that follow traditional patterns. Stith Thompson, author of *The Folktale* (1946), explains that traditional prose tales have been "handed down from generation to generation, either in writing or by word of mouth" (4). Older children tell tales to younger children, who in turn become members of the playground's "older generation."

Evelyn Pitcher and Ernst Prelinger analyze the narratives of very young children in their book *Children Tell Stories* (1963), which takes a psychoanalytic approach. Brian Sutton-Smith's more recent study *The Folkstories of Children* (1981) presents stories told by children between the ages of 2 and 10. Identifying plot elements that indicate varying levels of conflict resolution, Sutton-Smith finds that children cope with challenges through storytelling.

Some of the most popular tales are those that begin in a scary or spooky way and end with a funny or surprising line. Folklore scholars have given such narratives different names. Sylvia Grider calls them "folktales with catch endings"; John M. Vlach calls them "humorous anti-legends," while Simon J. Bronner prefers "playful horror tales" (154–59). When I did the fieldwork for my dissertation on preadolescent girls' storytelling, I found that the girls with whom I worked preferred their own term, *funny-scary story.* The two most common folktale patterns for stories of this kind are Aarne-Thompson tale types 326, "The Youth Who Wanted to Learn What Fear Is," and 366, "The Man from the Gallows."

Legends

Legends tell us about dangers and problems that may arise in our own lives. Linda Dégh, author of *Legend and Belief,* explains that the legend is "an ideology-sensitive genre par excellence." Based on issues and fears arising from contemporary society, "the legend has power, the nature of which is unknown and dangerous" (5). Since the legend adapts quickly to changing times, its potential for meaning remains powerful.

When children stay away from home overnight, their sensitivity to the legend's threats increases. At slumber parties and residential camps and in other unfamiliar settings, children feel more vulnerable to the tragic circumstances that legends portray. At camp, in particular, anxieties increase late at night. Who knows whether the sound of twigs breaking means the approach of a murderer, a ghost, or a harmless small animal? Folklorists' studies of camp legends, such as James P. Leary's "The Boondocks Monster of Camp Wapehani," Lee Haring and Mark Breslerman's "The Cropsey Maniac," and my own "Cropsey at Camp," have documented how children respond to such fearful stimuli. Simon J. Bronner includes camp legends in *American Children's Folklore* (153–54).

Folklorists have done more studies of camps than of other residential establishments where children tell legends. Jay Mechling's "Children's Folklore in Residential Institutions" (1995) reminds us to consider various organizations that "make the young person a 'ward' of the adult caretakers": orphanages, group homes, and detention centers (273). Bess Lomax Hawes's "'La Llorona' in Juvenile Hall" (1968) shows how legends about a ghostly mother/murderer reflect the worries of teenage girls detained for truancy and sexual misbehavior. In Jesse Gelwicks's "Redwood Grove: Youth Culture within a Group Home" (2002), storytelling about boys' past behavior follows legend-telling patterns. Institutions that provide medical treatment also serve as settings for storytelling, as Roberta Krell's "At a Children's Hospital" (1980) demonstrates.

Legends told in the first person ("This happened to me...") are called *memorates*. Carl Wilhelm von Sydow, who introduced this term, distinguished between memorates and *fabulates,* which are fictional narratives (65–80). Most contemporary legend specialists view memorates as part of the legend genre. Many children and adolescents tell first-person narratives related to legends; stories about legend trips (visits to haunted or otherwise extraordinary places featured in legends) usually describe the narrator's own experiences.

"The Dialectics of the Legend" (1973), by Linda Dégh and Andrew Vázsonyi, explains the legend's interplay of belief, partial belief, and skepticism. Debate and controversy help to keep the legend alive. Some young legend-tellers believe in the truth of the stories they tell, while others do not. How do legends spread from one group of people to another? In 1975, Linda Dégh and Andrew Vázsonyi published their essay "The Hypothesis of Multi-Conduit Transmission in Folklore." According to their hypothesis, folklore moves through social conduits. A conduit involves transmission of folklore from one interested person to another; some people neither tell nor listen to a piece of folklore, but others promote its transmission. Gary Alan Fine's essay "Folklore Diffusion through Interactive Social Networks: Conduits in a Preadolescent Community" (1979) applies the multi-conduit hypothesis to preadolescent boys living in a Minnesota suburb. Examining two narratives—one about a broken window at a local school and another about a child's death after eating Pop Rocks candy—Fine concludes that folklore spreads "only among sub-populations with particular interests or experience patterns, or according to group structures or friendship networks" (122).

The term *urban legend* became popular when Jan H. Brunvand published his first collection of legends for a general readership, *The Vanishing Hitchhiker* (1981). This collection and others by Brunvand, including *The Choking Doberman* (1984) and *The Baby Train* (1993), include stories told by adolescents. Some folklorists prefer the term *contemporary legend,* which does not specify urban settings.

RITUALS

Children often practice rituals, which can be defined as repeated patterns of behavior. Parents teach their children to follow certain rituals, such as bedtime routines, special meals, and holiday observances (Zeitlin, Kotkin, and Baker 162–81). Without guidance from adults, children practice their own rituals to make good things happen, initiate each other into clubs, celebrate holidays, and add excitement to their daily lives.

Rituals to get a day off from school are common in parts of the United States where heavy snowfall may cause a snow day. In upstate New York, children tell each other that wearing white socks to bed will guarantee a good snowstorm; hopeful children go to bed wearing snow-white tube socks. This ritual illustrates the principle of sympathetic magic: like produces like. Another ritual to produce snowstorms involves wearing pajamas inside-out or putting pajamas on backwards. Instead of a normal school day, with all of its challenges and frustrations, children hope to get an "inside-out" day that involves staying home, sleeping late, and having fun.

Initiation rituals emphasize the beginning of a new stage of life. Children have developed various rituals to bring new members into secret clubs or other groups in which adults have no involvement. Julius Cavero, a well-known graffiti artist born in New Jersey in 1961, joined the adolescent gang known as the "Bronx Enchanters" when he was in his early teens. To join the gang, he had to run between two lines of boys swinging belts and throwing punches. Once he had made it through this "Apache line" without falling down, he was a member of the gang. Later, when he decided to leave the Bronx Enchanters, Cavero had to undergo an exit ritual: 10 lashes from a gang member's belt (Cavero 12–13).

On Halloween, children practice rituals that they have learned from each other. Trick-or-treating on Halloween night is derived from ritual begging in the British Isles. Since the mid-1960s, children and adults have told stories about Halloween tragedies that have led to discouragement of neighborhood trick-or-treating (see the article "Halloween Poisonings"). Halloween is also associated with divination rituals such as mirror gazing, during which a girl tries to see the face of her future husband (Ellis 142–73).

Other rituals related to the supernatural can be practiced at any time of year. Ouija boards, which date back to the time of Pythagoras in ancient Greece,

Halloween trick-or-treaters in Maine, 2007. Photograph by Martha Harris.

provide a means for ritualized communication with the dead. Séances require no props; children sit in a circle, waiting for spirits' messages. "Bloody Mary" rituals involve summoning a spirit by repeating his or her name a certain number of times. For more details regarding folklore of the supernatural, see chapter 4.

MATERIAL CULTURE

Children's familiarity with material culture—the process of creating and using things—has resulted in the production of toys and shelters, as well as customs and beliefs associated with objects. Nature lore, understudied by contemporary folklorists, drew the attention of scholars in the nineteenth and early twentieth century. William Wells Newell discusses "flower oracles," including daisy petals and blades of grass, that foretell future spouses, in his *Games and Songs of American Children* 105–7). Alice Morse Earle's *Child Life in Colonial Days* (1900) describes children's nature play, including the creation of whistles and tea sets from natural objects. In 1987, Jeanne R. Chesanow published *Honeysuckle Sipping: The Plant Lore of Childhood,* based on interviews with adults who fondly remembered sipping "honey" from honeysuckle blossoms and interacting with nature in other traditional ways. Laura Watson's essay "The Nature Lore of Children: Functions and Variations" (1993) analyzes children's use of natural objects to make toys, games, and weapons. Examining an intriguing range of beliefs and practices related to nature, Watson concludes that "magic is the most important element of nature" (59).

Toys, defined by Bernard Mergen as "the material artifacts of play," include both homemade and store-bought items. Mergen observes that the Industrial Revolution gave children new playthings, including coat hangers, tires, rubber bands, tin cans, and bottle tops (103). From colonial times to the early twentieth century, children made many of their own playthings. The twentieth century's booming toy industry shifted children's focus to appealing mass-produced toys. In spite of the availability of commercially produced toys these days, many children enjoy making simple toys of their own. Some of the most common folk toys made by children include paper fortune-tellers (sometimes known as cootie catchers), paper footballs, slingshots, and pop-guns (Bronner 199–203).

According to the season, children build different outdoor shelters. In winter, snow forts and houses make good places to hide. Summertime creations include

Tree house built by three brothers in Logan, Utah, 2007. Photograph by Geoffrey Gould.

tree houses and other shelters made of salvaged materials. Some families' tree houses, built by a child or children over a period of years, become cherished artifacts of the family's growth.

WORKS CITED

Abrahams, Roger D. *Jump Rope Rhymes: A Dictionary.* Austin: American Folklore Society, 1969.

Abrahams, Roger, and Lois Rankin. *Counting-Out Rhymes: A Dictionary.* Austin: U of Texas P, 1980.

Ariès, Philippe. *Centuries of Childhood: A Social History of Family Life.* New York: Knopf, 1962.

Arleo, Andy. "Strategy in Counting-Out: Evidence from Saint-Nazaire, France." *Children's Folklore Review* 14.1 (1991): 25–29.

Armitage, Marc. "The Ins and Outs of School Playground Play: Children's Use of 'Play Places.'" *Play Today in the Primary School Playground.* Ed. Julia C. Bishop and Mavis Curtis. Buckingham, Eng.: Open UP, 2001. 37–58.

Ayers, Rick, ed. *Berkeley High School Slang Dictionary.* Berkeley: North Atlantic, 2004.

Beresin, Ann Richman. "Double Dutch and Double Cameras: Studying the Transmission of Culture in an Urban School Yard." *Children's Folklore: A Source Book.* Ed. Brian Sutton-Smith, Jay Mechling, Thomas W. Johnson, and Felicia R. McMahon. New York and London: Garland, 1995. 75–92.

Bishop, Julia, and Mavis Curtis, eds. *Play Today in the Primary School Playground.* Buckingham, Eng.: Open UP, 2001.

Bolton, H. C. *The Counting-Out Rhymes of Children.* New York: Appleton, 1888.

Bronner, Simon J. *American Children's Folklore.* Little Rock: August, 1988.

Brunvand, Jan H. *The Baby Train.* New York: Norton, 1993.

———. *The Choking Doberman.* New York: Norton, 1984.

———. *The Vanishing Hitchhiker.* New York: Norton, 1981.

Caillois, Roger. *Man, Play and Games.* New York: Free Press of Glencoe, 1961.

Cavero, Julius. *The Nasty Terrible T-Kid 170.* New York: From Here to Fame, 2006.

Chesanow, Jeanne R. *Honeysuckle Sipping: The Plant Lore of Childhood.* Camden, ME: Down East, 1987.

Cole, Joanna. *Yours Till Banana Splits: 201 Autograph Rhymes.* Minneapolis: Tandem, 1995.

Cooper, Martha. *Street Play.* New York: From Here to Fame, 2006.

Coughlan, Sean. "Texting Insults at Primary School." *BBC News.* April 7, 2003. http://news.bbc.co.uk/2/hi/uk_news/education/2925663.stm.

Dargan, Amanda, and Steven Zeitlin. *City Play.* New Brunswick, NJ: Rutgers UP, 1990.

Darian-Smith, Kate, and June Factor, eds. *Child's Play: Dorothy Howard and the Folklore of Australian Children.* Melbourne: Museum Victoria, 2005.

Dégh, Linda. *Legend and Belief.* Bloomington: Indiana UP, 2001.

Dégh, Linda, and Andrew Vázsonyi. "The Dialectics of the Legend." *Folklore Preprint Series* 1.6 (1973).

————. "The Hypothesis of Multi-Conduit Transmission in Folklore." *Folklore: Performance and Communication.* Ed. Dan Ben-Amos and Kenneth S. Goldstein. The Hague: Mouton, 1975. 207–51.

Douglas, Norman. *London Street Games.* 1916. London: Chatto and Windus, 1931.

Dundes, Alan. "On Game Morphology." *Readings in American Folklore.* Ed. Jan Harold Brunvand. New York: Norton, 1979. 334–44.

Earle, Alice Morse. *Child Life in Colonial Days.* New York: Macmillan, 1898.

Ellis, Bill. *Lucifer Ascending: The Occult in Folklore and Popular Culture.* Lexington: UP of Kentucky, 2004.

Factor, June. *Kidspeak: A Dictionary of Australian Children's Words, Expressions and Games.* Melbourne: U of Melbourne, 2000.

————. "Three Myths about Children's Folklore." *Play Today in the Primary School Playground.* Ed. Julia C. Bishop and Mavis Curtis. Buckingham, Eng., and Philadelphia: Open UP, 2001. 24–36.

Fine, Gary Alan. "Folklore Diffusion through Interactive Social Networks: Conduits in a Preadolescent Community." *New York Folklore* 5.1–2 (1979): 87–126.

Fraiberg, Selma. *The Magic Years.* New York: Scribner, 1959.

Freud, Sigmund. *Jokes and Their Relation to the Unconscious.* 1905. New York: Norton, 1963.

Gaunt, Kyra D. *The Games Black Girls Play: Learning the Ropes from Double-Dutch to Hip-Hop.* New York: New York UP, 2006.

Gelwicks, Jesse. "Redwood Grove: Youth Culture within a Group Home." *Children's Folklore Review* 24.1–2 (2002): 65–83.

Goldstein, Kenneth S. "Strategy in Counting Out: An Ethnographic Field Study." *The Study of Games.* Ed. Elliott M. Avedon and Brian Sutton-Smith. New York: Wiley, 1971. 167–78.

Gomme, Alice Bertha. *The Traditional Games of England, Scotland, and Ireland.* 2 vols. 1894–98. New York: Dover, 1964.

Green, Joanne, and J.D.A. Widdowson. *Traditional English Language Genres: Continuity and Change, 1950–2000.* Sheffield: National Centre for English Cultural Tradition, 2003.

Grider, Sylvia. "The Supernatural Narratives of Children." Dissertation, Indiana University, 1976.

Hall, Gary. "Folkgames." *Introduction to Folklore.* Ed. Robert J. Adams. Columbus: Collegiate, 1973. 70–79.

"Halloween Poisonings." *Urban Legends Reference Pages.* 2005. http://www.snopes.com/horrors/poison/halloween.asp.

Haring, Lee, and Mark Breslerman. "The Cropsey Maniac." *New York Folklore* 3.1–4 (1977): 15–27.

Hawes, Bess Lomax. "'La Llorona' in Juvenile Hall." *Western Folklore* 27.3 (1968): 153–70.

————. *Pizza Pizza Daddy-O.* Betacam tape. University of California at Berkeley, 1969.

Hellendoorn, Joop, Rimmert van der Kooij, and Brian Sutton-Smith, eds. *Play and Intervention.* Albany: SUNY Press, 1994.

Huizinga, Johan. *Homo Ludens.* 1938. Boston: Beacon, 1955.

Jorgensen, Marilyn. "Teases and Pranks." *Children's Folklore: A Source Book*. Ed. Brian Sutton-Smith, Jay Mechling, Thomas W. Johnson, and Felicia R. McMahon. New York and London: Garland, 1995. 213–24.

Kalliala, Marjatta. *Play Culture in a Changing World*. Maidenhead, Eng.: Open UP, 2006.

Kirshenblatt-Gimblett, Barbara, and Mary Sanches. "Children's Traditional Speech Play and Child Language." *Speech Play: Research and Resources for Studying Linguistic Creativity*. Ed. Barbara Kirshenblatt-Gimblett. Philadelphia: U of Pennsylvania P, 1976.

Knapp, Mary and Herbert. *One Potato, Two Potato: The Secret Education of American Children*. New York: Norton, 1976.

Krell, Roberta. "At a Children's Hospital: A Folklore Survey." *Western Folklore* 39 (1980): 223–31.

Lash, Sarah. "Situating Puzzles: Exploring a Neglected Genre." *Midwest Folklore* 31.2 (2005): 15–38.

Leary, James P. "The Boondocks Monster of Camp Wapehani." *Indiana Folklore* 6.2 (1973): 174–90.

Mansfield, Susan. "Sonic Takes on the Dusty Bluebells." *The Big Issue in Scotland* 95 (November 21–27, 1996): 24–25.

McDowell, John H. *Children's Riddling*. Bloomington: Indiana UP, 1979.

McNeil, William K. "From Advice to Laments: New York Autograph Album Verse, 1850–1900." *New York Folklore Quarterly* 26 (1970): 163–203.

Mechling, Jay. "Children's Folklore in Residential Institutions: Summer Camps, Boarding Schools, Hospitals, and Custodial Facilities." *Children's Folklore: A Source Book*. Ed. Brian Sutton-Smith, Jay Mechling, Thomas W. Johnson, and Felicia R. McMahon. New York and London: Garland, 1995. 273–92.

———. *On My Honor: Boy Scouts and the Making of American Youth*. Chicago and London: U of Chicago P, 2001.

Mergen, Bernard. *Play and Playthings*. Westport: Greenwood, 1982.

Newell, William Wells. *Games and Songs of American Children*. 1883. New York: Dover, 1963.

Olsen, Stefanie. "Cracking the Code of Teens' IM Slang." *CNET News.com*. November 14, 2006. http://news.com/2009–1025_3-613547.html.

Opie, Iona, and Peter Opie. *Children's Games in Street and Playground*. Oxford: Clarendon, 1969.

———. *I Saw Esau: Traditional Rhymes of Youth*. London: Williams and Norgate, 1947.

———. *The Lore and Language of Schoolchildren*. New York: Oxford UP, 1959.

———. *Oxford Dictionary of Nursery Rhymes*. 1951. Oxford: Clarendon, 1973.

———. *The Singing Game*. New York: Oxford UP, 1985.

"Origins of Rock, Paper, Scissors (Jan Ken Pon)." *Hwacha*. September 9, 2006. http://www.hwacha.net/janken_origins.

Oring, Elliott. "On the Tradition and Mathematics of Counting-Out." *Western Folklore* 56.2 (1997): 139–52.

Pellegrini, Anthony D., ed. *The Future of Play Theory*. New York: SUNY Press, 1995.

Piaget, Jean. *Play, Dreams, and Imitation in Childhood*. New York: Norton, 1972.

Pitcher, Evelyn, and Ernst Prelinger. *Children Tell Stories*. New York: International Universities Press, 1963.

Posen, I. Sheldon. "Pranks and Practical Jokes at Children's Summer Camps." *Southern Folklore Quarterly* 38 (1974): 299–309.

Powell, Azizi. "Foot Stomping Cheers." *Cocojams.com*. 2001. http://www.cocojams.com/foot_stomping_cheers.htm.

Roemer, Danielle. "Riddles." *Children's Folklore: A Source Book*. Ed. Brian Sutton-Smith, Jay Mechling, Thomas W. Johnson, and Felicia R. McMahon. New York and London: Garland, 1995. 161–92.

Samuelson, Sue. "A Review of the Distinctive Genres of Adolescent Folklore." *Children's Folklore Review* 17.2 (1995): 13–31.

Schwartzman, Helen. *Transformations: The Anthropology of Children's Play*. New York: Plenum, 1978.

Sherman, Josepha. "Gopher Guts and Army Trucks: The Modern Evolution of Children's Folklore." *Children's Folklore Review* 21.2 (1999): 17–24.

Sherman, Josepha, and T.K.F. Weisskopf. *Greasy Grimy Gopher Guts: The Subversive Folklore of Childhood*. Little Rock: August, 1995.

Simons, Elizabeth Radin. "The NASA Joke Cycle: The Astronauts and the Teacher." *Western Folklore* 45 (October 1986): 261–77.

Singer, Jerome L. *The Child's World of Make-Believe*. New York: Academic Press, 1973.

Sullivan, C. W. III. "Songs, Poems, and Rhymes." *Children's Folklore: A Source Book*. Ed. Brian Sutton-Smith, Jay Mechling, Thomas W. Johnson, and Felicia R. McMahon. New York and London: Garland, 1995. 145–60.

Sutton-Smith, Brian. "A Developmental Structural Account of Riddles." *Speech Play: Research and Resources for Studying Linguistic Creativity*. Ed. Barbara Kirshenblatt-Gimblett. Philadelphia: U of Pennsylvania P, 1976. 111–19.

———. *The Folkstories of Children*. Philadelphia: U of Pennsylvania P, 1981.

———. "The Kissing Games of Adolescents in Ohio." 1959. *The Folkgames of Children*. Ed. Brian Sutton-Smith. Austin: U of Texas P, 1972. 465–90.

Tallman, Richard S. "A Generic Approach to the Practical Joke." *Southern Folklore Quarterly* 38 (1974): 259–74.

Thomas, Jeannie B. "Dumb Blondes, Dan Quayle, and Hillary Clinton: Gender, Sexuality, and Stupidity in Jokes." *Journal of American Folklore* 110.437 (1997): 277–313.

Thompson, Stith. *The Folktale*. New York: Holt, Rinehart and Winston, 1946.

Toelken, Barre. *The Dynamics of Folklore*. Boston: Houghton, 1979.

Tucker, Elizabeth. "Cropsey at Camp." *Voices: The Journal of New York Folklore* 32.3–4 (2006): 42.

Virtanen, Leea. *Children's Lore*. Studia Fennica 22. Helsinki: Suomalisen Kirjallisuuden Seura, 1978.

Vlach, John M. "One Black Eye and Other Horrors: A Case for the Humorous Anti-Legend." *Indiana Folklore* 4 (1971): 95–140.

Von Sydow, Carl Wilhelm. *Selected Papers on Folklore*. Copenhagen: Rosenkilde and Bagger, 1948.

Watson, Laura. "The Nature Lore of Children: Functions and Variations." *Children's Folklore Review* 16.1 (1993): 49–60.

Widdowson, J.D.A. "Rhythm, Repetition and Rhetoric: Learning Language in the School Playground." *Play Today in the Primary School Playground.* Ed. Julia C. Bishop and Mavis Curtis. Buckingham, Eng., and Philadelphia: Open UP, 2001. 135–51.

Zehr, Mary Ann. "Panic over Anthrax Spreads to Schools." *Dubuque Community School District Web Work Groups.* October 24, 2001. http://www.dubuque.k12.ia.us/crteam/index.htm.

Zeitlin, Steven J., Amy J. Kotkin, and Holly Cutting Baker. *A Celebration of American Family Folklore.* Cambridge, MA: Yellow Moon, 1982.

Three
Examples and Texts

This chapter presents children's folklore that was published or collected from the early twentieth century to the first decade of the twenty-first century. Sources include folklore archives, journals, books, dissertations, and Web sites. Some of the material comes from my own fieldwork in Indiana, Maine, and New York. When possible, I include information about informants' ethnicities. Most child informants have pseudonyms; the few names come from publications, archives, and Web sites.

Children's folklore surveys since the mid-twentieth century have focused primarily on verbal lore, rituals, and games, but some have considered material culture as well. Simon J. Bronner's *American Children's Folklore* (1988) begins with folk speech, rhymes, songs, riddles, and jokes and then covers narratives, customs, rituals, games, toys, and other forms of material culture. This handbook follows a similar sequence. For the greatest possible accessibility, this chapter follows the same order as that of the children's folklore genres in chapter 2. Since chapter 2 includes many examples of speech play, that genre does not appear here.

RIDDLES, JOKES, AND ROUTINES OF VICTIMIZATION

Riddles

What has a tongue and it can't talk?—a shoe.

What has four legs and can't walk?—a chair.

A thousand lights in a dish, what is it?—stars.

Playtime at a preschool in Jamaica, 2006. Photograph by Geoffrey Gould.

What's black and white and red all over?—a skunk with a heat rash.

White from the outside, green from the inside—a frog sandwich.

These riddles come from John H. McDowell's 1975 dissertation, "The Speech Play and Verbal Art of Chicano Children: An Ethnographic and Sociolinguistic Study" (104–05). Eight-year-old girls told the first four riddles; the teller of the last one was an eight-year-old boy.

The first two riddles confuse the listener through apparent antithesis, while the last three offer insufficient details to come up with the correct answer. "A thousand lights in a dish" is an appealing but confusing metaphor. As Mac E. Barrick observes, "What's black and white and red all over?" has circulated actively in the childhood underground, with a variety of answers. Comparable riddling questions can be found in Knapp and Knapp (106–11) and Bronner (116).

Why did the chicken cross the road? To get to the other side!

Why did the turkey cross the road? To prove he wasn't chicken!

Four-and-a-half-year-old Mathew Baker told these riddles to his sister, student collector Courtney Hutchins, in Salt Lake City, Utah, in the spring of 2001.

Riddling questions like these express young children's desire to learn and their love of linguistic tricks. "Why did the chicken cross the road?" is a catch riddle with a deceptively simple answer; "Why did the turkey cross the road?" takes that riddle one step farther, with a humorous twist. Folklorists of childhood have tended to identify the prime age for riddle telling as seven to nine, but Mathew's enthusiastic riddle telling shows that some younger children tell riddles very well.

> How do you know a blonde has been at her computer? There's Tippex [correction fluid] all over the screen.

This riddle-joke from a fifth-grade boy (9–10 years old) in Ireland comes from the data sample of Sara Staunton, whose "Riddle Use and Comprehension in Irish School-Aged Children: A Developmental Study" was published in 2001 (99). "Dumb blonde" riddle-jokes have been popular in the United States and in Ireland since the 1990s. According to Jeannie B. Thomas, blondes stereotypically seem to be slow-witted but attractive and eager to please.

> How did the computer criminal get out of jail? He pressed the escape key!
>
> Why did the computer cross the road? Because the chicken programmed it to.
>
> What do you call an elephant that takes a bite out of the computer? A megabyte!

Children in different parts of the world sent these three riddle-jokes to Barbara J. Feldman, administrator of http://www.jokesbykids.com, in 2006 and 2007. The first came from 10-year-old Joseph in Singapore, the second came from 9-year-old Blake in Australia, and the third came from 12-year-old Courtney in the United States. Both the second and the third riddle reference well-established riddles about animals that have made children laugh since the twentieth century (Bronner 125–27).

> What is black and white and has wheels? A panda on roller skates!

Eight-year-old Kirsten, who lives in Eau Claire, Wisconsin, sent me her favorite riddle on e-mail in February 2008. Riddles that begin with the words "What is black and white…" offer children endless possibilities for classifying people, animals, and things in humorous ways. Many answers to this riddling question can be found on the Internet. Early in 2008, a Google search of the riddle's first six words generated 369,000 hits.

Jokes

Knock Knock!

> Knock knock. Who's there? Wayne. Wayne who? Wayne drops keep falling on my head.
>
> Knock knock. Who's there? Lettuce. Lettuce who? Lettuce in and you'll find out.

Knock knock. Who's there? Grandma. Grandma who? Grandma. Knock knock. Who's there? Grandma. Grandma who? Grandma [repeat this 3 or 4 times]. Knock knock. Who's there? Aunt. Aunt who? Aren't you glad I got rid of all the grandmas?

Heather Russell collected these three knock-knock jokes from children on a multicultural playground in Melbourne, Australia, in 1986 (78). A Turkish girl in grade six told the first joke, a Chinese boy in grade four told the second, and a girl of English-speaking background in grade five told the third.

Knock-knock jokes encourage elementary-school children to demonstrate their linguistic skills. Most knock-knock jokes make people laugh through perfect or imperfect puns. Not all children tell knock-knock jokes smoothly; while some jokes of this kind sound awkward, all of them facilitate a learning process. For more knock-knock jokes, see Knapp and Knapp (94) and Bronner (118–19).

Honda-Honda

There was this guy, and every time he farted it would come out "Honda-Honda." He was getting pretty embarrassed, so he went to the doctor to find out what was wrong. The doctor couldn't find anything wrong with him, so he sent him to a Japanese dentist. So the guy went to the dentist.

When he got there, the dentist goes (Japanese accent), "Mister, you got an abscess!" And the guy goes "What? What does an abscess have to do with me farting Honda-Honda?" And the dentist says, "You dummy, don't you know abscess makes the fart go Honda?"

Twelve-year-old Mary told this joke in Vestal, New York, in April 1978. With its reversal of consonants and alteration of syllables, Mary's joke fits the patterns of the shaggy dog story and the spoonerism. The word "fart" pleases preadolescents who are keenly aware of their maturing bodies and rules for polite social interaction.

Blowing Bubbles

One day there was this class, and there were children in it listening to the teacher. The teacher got mad if anyone was ever late. Well, you see Johnny was late, and he walked in and the teacher says, "Where were you, Johnny?" He said that he was outside blowing bubbles. The teacher scolded him and said not to be late again. Then you see, Billy walked in late and the teacher asked him where he was and he said that he was blowing bubbles. The teacher, you see, scolded him too. Then a little time passed, and in walked this little girl. The teacher asked her who she was. And well, this little girl said, "Hi, I'm Bubbles."

Ten-year-old Gillian told this joke in Huntington, New York, in March 1979. Like many of the jokes in the first chapter of Gershon Legman's *Rationale of the Dirty Joke,* this one introduces children who seem innocent but prove to be more sophisticated. While jokes of this kind make listeners laugh, they also suggest that children know more about sex than their elders think they do.

Helen Keller

Did you see Helen Keller's new car? Neither did she!

How come you can't hear Helen Keller in the winter? Because she wears mittens.

Two teenagers swapped Helen Keller jokes in the library of their high school in Smithtown, New York, in April 1987. Fourteen-year-old Kathy told the first joke; 15-year-old Brent told the second one. Both Kathy and Brent identified themselves as "brains" (high achievers), in contrast to "jocks" and "burnouts." After telling Helen Keller jokes, both Kathy and Brent told several ethnic jokes.

Jokes about disabled individuals, many of which fit the popular riddle-joke format, break rules about showing respect for people who have physical challenges. Why do kids joke about Helen Keller (1880–1968), the highly admired author who had been deaf and blind since early childhood? Her status as a heroic activist for the rights of the disabled makes her an obvious—though inappropriate—target for children's humor. Some people feel anxious about the possibility of becoming disabled. Jokes provide an outlet for this anxiety, making it possible to laugh at a subject that has no intrinsic humorous value. For other Helen Keller jokes, see Bronner (128–29).

Stop Sign

There was this Polack, a German guy and an Italian guy, they are on a big hill. So then they are going down the hill and the Italian guy goes, "We have no brakes!" The German guy goes, "How are we going to stop?" and the Polack guy goes, "Well, there is a stop sign at the end—we'll stop!"

Thirteen-year-old David, a middle-school student of Polish descent, told this joke in Endwell, New York, in April 1978. When asked why he liked to tell Polish jokes, David replied, "Polish jokes are really funny; everyone laughs at them." In the spring of 1978, the Polish joke cycle was flourishing; the election of the highly respected Polish Pope John Paul II in October of that year made Polish jokes even more popular. Although Polish jokes began as jabs at Polish immigrants, they quickly became "numskull" jokes with minimal intent to criticize. Other ethnic jokes can be found in Bronner (121–23) and Knapp and Knapp (204–06).

April Fool

A boy came running in to his mother and said, "Mother, Mother, pappa has hung himself in the attic." "Oh, no, what do you mean, has he hung himself in the attic?" She ran up

Boys tell jokes in their New York City clubhouse in the late 1970s. Photograph by Martha Cooper.

but came down right away and said, "You are lying, boy. He hasn't hung himself in the attic." Then he said, "April fool, Mother, he hung himself in the basement."

This sick or tasteless joke, collected from an 11-year-old boy in Norway, was published in Reimund Kvideland's essay "Stories about Death as a Part of Children's Socialization" (1980). The joke's punch line resembles the punch lines of some jokes in the "dead-baby" joke cycle. Although the boy's reaction to his father's death seems flippant and uncaring, it reflects children's need to come to terms with the reality of death.

Routines of Victimization

Did You Get It?

Melissa: Darla, come here! I wrote this letter to you on Tuesday. Did you get it?

Darla: Nope.

Melissa: [stamps Darla's foot] I guess I forgot to stamp it.

Nine-year-old Melissa demonstrated this routine for folklorist Danielle Roemer in 1977 (66). Roemer identifies two roles for participants in routines like this one: trickster and straight man. As trickster, Melissa sets up a situation where mild victimization can take place. Since the pronoun "it" has many possible referents, there is some leeway for interpretation here.

Did You Kill Your Mother?

Hold your hand out and turn one finger down every time you answer "no" to a question. Start with the finger that's farthest away from your thumb.

> Did you kill your mother? (No)
>
> Did you kill your father? (No)
>
> Did you kill your gramma? (No)
>
> Then what are you doing with a gun in your hand?

Seven-year-old Paul taught me this routine in the spring of 1996 while visiting my introductory folklore class with his mother. After I turned down my little finger and the next two fingers, the only digits still extended were the thumb and the adjacent finger: children's traditional representation of a gun. In a culture where guns frequently appear on TV, it is not surprising to discover a child's routine that leaves the victim with a gun. Such routines mirror society's concern about violence; they also let the child take the role of a clever detective. *IDK, pretty true*

Slap Me Five

> Slap me five (high-five clap)
> Slap me low (low clap)
> Slap me middle (swipe hand toward middle very quickly, then remove it)
> You're too slow

Robert, an Anglo-American sixth-grader in Vestal, New York, shared this routine with me in the winter of 1998. The influence of hip-hop culture is clear here. Although the routine begins with a friendly high-five, it ends with a putdown (Green and Widdowson 363). *What?! Lol*

RHYMES

Counting-Out Rhymes

Intie, Mintie

Intie, Mintie,
Tibbity Fee, Delia, Delia, Dominee,
Icha, Picha, Dominicha,
Alka, Palka, Poo,
Out pops Y-O-U.

Intie, Mintie, Tootsa, Lala,
Falama Linkie, Dinkie, Dala,
Falama Lee, Falama Loo,
Out pops Y-O-U.

Nola Johnson, a student at the University of Maine, recorded both of these counting-out rhymes in January 1967. She learned the first rhyme from her mother and the second from her father. Both of her parents grew up in a Swedish neighborhood of Worcester, Massachusetts. These two counting-out rhymes represent the many variants of Intie, Mintie that have circulated in the British Isles and the United States (Abrahams and Rankin 122–25; Opie and Opie, *Oxford Dictionary* 224; Newell 200).

O-R-A-N-G-E

Serena: Cabbage patch, cabbage patch in a dish,
What color hair do you wish?
And say Dori said 'orange,' then you'd go O-R-A-N-G-E spells orange.

Dori: My mother and your mother live across the street
1918 Alligator Street
And every night they have a fight and this is what they say:
Boys are rotten, made out of cotton,
Girls are sexy, made out of Pepsi.
With a cherry, cherry dish rag on your big fat toe, and that means you're
not IT.

Serena and Dori, both eight years old, recited these two rhymes in Binghamton, New York, in April 1987. Both rhymes have circulated actively in oral tradition. The first, which more commonly begins with the line "Bubble gum, bubble gum in a dish," can be traced back to 1927; the second, which often takes the form of a clapping game, can be traced back to 1888 (Abrahams and Rankin 28, 154; Bronner 53). Humorous lines distinguishing boys from girls were very popular in the 1980s and 1990s, reflecting girls' awareness of changing gender roles.

Ip Dip Do

Ip dip do,
Cat's got flu,
Dog's got chicken-pox
Out goes you

Joanne Green and J.D.A. Widdowson include this counting-out rhyme in their *Traditional English Language Genres: Continuity and Change, 1950–2000* (367).

The two most popular counting-out rhymes in their data sample are One Potato, Two Potato and Ip Dip Do. A variant of Ip Dip Do appeared in the summer of 1953, when Queen Elizabeth II was crowned in England: "Red, white, and blue, / The Queen's got the flu, / The King's got the tummy ache / And don't know what to do" (Opie and Opie, *Lore and Language* 106).

Handclapping Rhymes

Apples on a Stick

Zing, zing, zing
Apples on a stick makes me sick
Makes my stomach go two forty-six
Not because it's dirty, not because it's clean,
Just because I kissed a boy behind the magazine.
Hey, kids, you wanna have a fight?
Here comes Wade, and Arron in sight.
They can wiggle and wobble and do the splits,
But most of all they can kiss, kiss, kiss.

Randall Hansen collected this rhyme from six-year-old Nate Hansen, who played clapping games in kindergarten at Santa Clara Elementary School in Utah in the summer of 1982. Roger D. Abrahams cites a 1948 version of this rhyme from West Virginia in *Jump-Rope Rhymes: A Dictionary* (11). Irene Chagall notes in her essay "Let's Get Rhythm" (2005–06) that the rhyme's opening lines "metaphorically refer to sexual intercourse" (46). See also Barbara Michaels and Bettye Whyte's *Apples on a Stick: The Folklore of Black Children* (1983).

Miss Sue, Miss Sue

Miss Sue, Miss Sue, Miss Sue from Alabama,
Sitting in a rocking chair, eating Betty Crocker,
Watching the clock go,
Tick-tock, tick-tock, banana rock,
Tick-tock, tick-tock, banana rock,
A-B-C-D-E-F-G, wash those spots right off of me.
Moonshine, moonshine. FREEZE!

This handclapping rhyme came from an informant in Fort Bragg, California, in 1994 (Folklore Archives, University of California at Berkeley). The word "FREEZE" signals that movement must suddenly stop. Irene Chagall notes that John and Alan Lomax collected versions of this rhyme in Alabama and Louisiana in 1934; she also discusses film and video documentation, which enables field-workers to preserve handclapping games' melodies and movements (52).

Miss Suzy

Miss Suzy was a baby, a baby, a baby, Miss Suzy was a baby, and this is
what she said! "ooh, aah, ooh aah aah!" (pretend to suck your thumbs, once each
  word)
Miss Suzy was a schoolgirl, a schoolgirl, a schoolgirl! Miss Suzy was a
schoolgirl, and this is what she said! "ooh, aah, ooh aah aah!" (flip your hair
back over your shoulders once each word)
Miss Suzy was a teenager, a teenager, a teenager, Miss Suzy was a teenager,
and this is what she said! "ooh, aah, I lost my bra! I left it in my boyfriend's
car!"
Miss Suzy was a teacher, a teacher, a teacher,
Miss Suzy was a teacher, and this is what she said! "ooh, aah, ooh aah aah!"
(shake your finger once each word)
Miss Suzy was a mother, a mother, a mother,
Miss Suzy was a mother, and this is what she said! "ooh, aah, ooh aah aah!"
(rock a pretend baby in your arms)
Miss Suzy was a grandmother, a grandmother, a grandmother, Miss Suzy
was a grandmother, and this is what she said! "ooh, aah, ooh aah aah!" (rock
in a pretend rocking chair)
Miss Suzy went to heaven, to heaven, to heaven, Miss Suzy went to heaven,
and this is what she said! "ooh, aah, ooh aah aah!" (flap your "wings")
Miss Suzy went to he-ell, to he-ell, to he-ell, Miss Suzy went to he-ell, and
this is what she said! "ooh, aah, ooh aah aah!" (pretend to be poked by a
pitchfork at each word)

Eighteen-year-old Lizzi (screenname) posted this handclapping rhyme on the discussion board at http://www.streetplay.com on May 1, 2000. In an earlier post-
ing, she had explained that she had learned handclapping rhymes in the 1980s.
    Andy Arleo's essay "The Saga of Susie" (2001) analyzes versions of this rhyme
collected from around the world. Documented in the Opies' 1985 study *The
Singing Game* (458), the rhyme delights children with its risqué humor and repetition. For more details on Arleo's study, see chapter 4.

Xena

Xena (clap) Warrior (clap) Princess,
Came here last year.
Xena Warrior Princess came here last year.
Over, over, over.

This handclapping rhyme was published in Janice Ackerley's collection of New
Zealand children's folklore in the newsletter *Play and Folklore* in September 2002.
The American television series *Xena, Warrior Princess,* filmed in New Zealand,
was on television from 1995 to 2001; clearly the children were proud that a
popular series had been filmed in their homeland. Ackerley notes that this hand-
clap served as a "starter" for the game of Paper, Scissors, Rock.

Eenie-Meenie

Eenie-meenie sissallini, ooh-whop-bop-a-lini
Atchi-katchi, liverachi, I hate boys,
Give me a peach, give me a plum,
Give me a stick of bubble gum
No peach, no plum, just a stick of bubble gum.

Sara Miller, who learned this handclapping rhyme at a day camp in the New York City area in the mid-1990s, recorded its text in April 2007, noting that it had almost the same words as J. J. Fad's 1988 song "Eenie Meenie Beats" (3). J. J. Fad's song does not include the words "I hate boys," which come from girls' interaction in the childhood underground. "Eenie-meenie" and "each, peach, plum" frequently appear in children's rhymes (Opie and Opie, *Lore and Language* 115; Knapp and Knapp 132–33; Armor). In *The Games Black Girls Play* (2006), Kyra D. Gaunt analyzes this rhyme in detail (89–93).

Jump-Rope Rhymes

Lizzie Borden

Lizzie Borden took an axe
And gave her mother forty whacks.   *This is crazy*
When she saw what she had done,
She gave her father forty-one

My father, Frank H. Tucker, professor emeritus at Colorado College, recited this rhyme in August 2006. As a sixth-grader in Wilmington, Delaware, in 1933, he heard girls chant this rhyme while jumping rope.

On August 4, 1892, Andrew and Abby Borden were murdered with an axe in their home in Fall River, Massachusetts. Their daughter Lizzie was tried and found not guilty of murder, but many people believed that Lizzie had killed her father and stepmother. In an effort to sell newspapers, a journalist wrote the above rhyme, which rapidly became part of children's folklore. Although Lizzie Borden tried to stay out of the public eye after her trial, children followed her around, chanting the "Lizzie Borden" rhyme.

A daughter's brutal murder of her parents reflects a dramatic role reversal; instead of respecting her parents' authority, she puts an end to their lives. It is not unusual for children to sing about killing parents, teachers, and other adults in songs such as the well-known parody of the "Battle Hymn of the Republic."

Pepsi Co

Pepsi co, Pepsi co,
When will we go to Mexico?
Never, never

Because we don't have money.
Who has money
Bathes in the sea;
Who doesn't have it
At home in a wash pan.

Folklorist Richard March collected this rhyme while watching girls play *gumi-gumi* (generally called Elastics or Chinese jump rope in English-speaking countries) in a parking lot in Velika Gorika, Croatia, in the spring of 1978; he translated the rhyme from Croatian to English.

This rhyme's content shows a sharp awareness of class distinctions. The girls, residents of a working-class suburb of Zagreb, knew that their families did not have enough money for lavish trips to the beach or to other countries. Jumping rope with a two-meter-long piece of elastic fastened to their ankles, calves, knees, or waists, they expressed their understanding of economics.

Gypsy, Gypsy

Gypsy, gypsy, please tell me
What my husband is going to be
Rich man, poor man, beggar man, thief,
Doctor, lawyer, Indian chief,
Butcher, baker, candlestick maker,
Tinker, tailor, cowboy, sailor

Utah State University student Kathleen Hamby, age 20, recited this jump-rope rhyme to student collector Jan Taggert in the spring of 1982.

Variants of this rhyme, documented in Abrahams's *Jump-Rope Rhymes: A Dictionary* (168–69), show how common it was for twentieth-century girls to guess a future husband's occupation. If a girl missed a skip, her last word indicated the occupation of her husband-to-be. Kathleen Hamby told her friend Jan Taggert that she and her friends would "just die" if they landed on either "poor man" or "Indian chief." Although the rhyme is playful, disrespect for Native Americans and hope for an affluent lifestyle come through.

If I Dare

Salt, vinegar, mustard, pepper,
If I dare, I can do better
Who says no 'cos hens don't crow
Salt, vinegar, mustard, pepper
Salt, vinegar, mustard, pepper
I wanna be great

A hot shot lawyer
A famous dancer
A tough operator
Salt, vinegar, mustard, pepper

Dan Jones collected this rhyme from Louise at the Vietnamese Community Centre in East London. This rhyme and others inspired Jones's large painting "The Singing Playground," created at the Victoria and Albert Museum of Childhood in London in 2004. The museum's Web site "The Singing Playground" includes rhyme transcripts and sound recordings, as well as a photograph of the painting. Lady Alice Gomme collected a version of this jump-rope rhyme in 1898 (2: 204), and many other versions have emerged since then (Abrahams 175–76).

Autograph Rhymes

When You Get Married

When you get married
And your old man gets cross,
Just pick up the broom
And show him who's boss.

When you get married
And have squalling brats,
Just cut off their heads
And feed 'em to the cats.

Life is like a rose,
Love is like a blossom.
If you want your finger bit,
Stick it at a possum.

These delightful autograph rhymes come from Vance Randolph and May Kennedy McCord's 1948 essay "Autograph Albums in the Ozarks" (182–93), which analyzes album entries from the late 1800s to the late 1940s in Missouri and Arkansas. Like many other autograph rhymes, these three give the book's owner advice for the future. The first two rhymes' messages seem facetious, but their focus on independence from husbands and children has a feminist orientation. The third rhyme effectively deflates the sentimentality favored by autograph rhyme writers of that period.

If All the Boys...

If all the boys
Lived across the sea,
Oh, what a swimmer
Libby would be!

When you get old
And think you're sweet,
Pull off your shoes
And smell your feet.

Two sixth-grade classmates wrote these rhymes in my autograph book in the spring of 1960 at John Eaton Elementary School in Washington, D.C. Sixth-graders, on the cusp of adolescence, wonder and worry about future social relationships. Autograph rhymes like these remind children not to take themselves too seriously. They also provoke laughter at a time of transition, when social relationships can seem complex and intimidating. For more examples of autograph rhymes, see Bronner (89–90).

Bad Future, Bad Luck

Calling car one, calling car two,
A pig named Sally escaped from the zoo!

God made the rivers, God made the lakes,
But when He made you He made a big MISTAKE!

Remember the trees and remember the grass,
Remember the days I kicked your ass!

Hope you have a bad future and bad luck in all you do.
Your favorite sister, Mei Mei

Susan Yee, a Chinese American student at Binghamton University, copied these verses from her sister Sally's autograph book in New York City in May 1980. Mei Mei, their youngest sister, had written these mocking verses in 1975, when she was 10. Sally considered Mei-Mei's verses to be among the best in her autograph book, because they made her friends laugh.

TAUNTS AND COUNTERTAUNTS

Baby, Baby

Baby, baby, stick your head in gravy,
Stir it around, stir it around,
You'll never get in the Navy.

This variant of the popular "Baby, Baby" taunt came from seven-year-old Celia in Watertown, New York, in the spring of 1979. Celia was taunting her brother, one year younger than herself. The Opies note one variant of this taunt in *I Saw Esau* (30) and more in *Lore and Language* (187–88); Edith Fowke includes a variant in *Sally Go Round the Sun* (116).

Cry-Baby Cow

Cry-baby cow, give [me/us] some milk.
How much does it cost?
Two nickels.

Halina Weiss presents this withering taunt in her essay *"Draznilkas*—Russian Children's Taunts" (1999). Like the English "Baby, Baby" taunt, this one mocks children for crying and encourages more mature behavior.

Snot-Nose

I am a stupid Snowmaiden,
Uncle Frost is my daddy,
My mother is a violet,
And you are a snot-nose.

Like the above verse, this countertaunt comes from Halina Weiss's 1999 essay on Russian children's insults. Weiss notes that the speaker, a girl who was accused of being stupid, turns the taunt around, so that the child who insulted her becomes a "snot-nose."

I'm Rubber

I'm rubber, you're glue, whatever you say bounces off of me and sticks to you.

Eight-year-old Molly responded to nine boys' taunts with this classic counter-taunt in Binghamton, New York, in April 1987. Iona and Peter Opie observe that "In any juvenile exchange of pleasantries the esteemed feature seems to be not the quality of the wit, but the ability to have the last word" (*Lore and Language* 45). Besides stopping criticism, this rhyme quasi-magically sends hurtful taunts back to the child who uttered them.

Liar, Liar

Liar, liar, pants on fire,
Hanging by a telephone wire.
While you're there, cut your hair
And stick it down your underwear.

Kellie Greenhalgh, a 20-year-old student at Utah State University, shared this taunt with Stephanie Smedley in the spring of 1998. Edith Fowke recognizes this taunt's popularity in Canada (114); Mary and Herbert Knapp identify it as a wide-spread American jeer (60). In 1997, the movie *Liar, Liar* gave the taunt's opening words another dimension of fame.

SONGS

Glory, Glory Hallelujah

Mine eyes have seen the glory of the burning of the school
We have tortured every teacher, we have broken every rule
We have planned to hang the principal, we boarded up the school
Our troops go marching on.
Glory, glory hallelujah, teacher hit me with the ruler
I met her at the door with a loaded 44
And she ain't my teacher no more—
I WONDER WHYYYYYY (Hand held over mouth to make "wah-wah" sound).

German American Erika V. Gimple collected this song parody from her 12-year-old daughter, Kathryn, who was singing in the car on the way to her first day of junior high school in September 1981 in Springfield, Virginia (Northern Virginia Folklife Center, George Mason University, item 1981–030). Since Kathryn was on her way to the first day of junior high school, her singing of this popular parody of "The Battle Hymn of the Republic" helped to express "back to school" jitters. Versions of this song parody appear in the Opies' *Lore and Language of Schoolchildren* (374), as well as more recent publications (Knapp and Knapp 173–74; Bronner 97–99).

On Top of Spaghetti

On top of spaghetti, all covered in blood,
I shot my poor teacher with a M 16 slug.
I shot her with pleasure, I shot her with pride,
I couldn't have missed her, she was 20 feet wide.
I went to her funeral, I went to her grave,
Some people threw flowers, I threw a grenade!

Janice Ackerley collected this parody of "On Top of Old Smoky" from New Zealand children between 1993 and 2003 ("Gender Issues" 34–35). Asking whether the extreme violence in songs like this one should be taken seriously, Ackerley notes that violent acts against teachers may warrant alarm (35); however, children's songs about tormenting their teachers often release tension and provoke laughter. Mary and Herbert Knapp include variants of "On Top of Old Smoky" in *One Potato, Two Potato* (174–76).

Barney

I hate you, you hate me,
Let's hang Barney from a tree.
With a shotgun, boom, right in the head,
Now that purple thing is dead.

I hate you, you hate me,
Let's gang up and kill Barney.
With a shotgun, boom, Barney's on the floor.
No more purple dinosaur.

I hate you, you hate me,
Barney died from HIV.
We called the doctor and the doctor said,
"Sorry, kids, Barney's dead."

Eight-year-old Robert, an elementary-school student of Anglo-American descent, sang these songs for me in Binghamton, New York, in October 1993. During that fall, children all over the United States were singing parodies of the theme song of the television show *Barney and Friends*. While very young children enjoyed Barney's antics, older children found his songs and actions to be insipid and ridiculous. Robert's first two parodies of Barney's theme song excoriate this icon of preschool popular culture; the third parody expresses a reaction to the AIDS epidemic, often in the news during that time period. For more details about the Barney song parody cycle, see my "'I Hate You, You Hate Me': Children's Responses to Barney the Dinosaur" (1999) and Josepha Sherman and T.K.F. Weisskopf's *Greasy Grimy Gopher Guts* (192–200).

Diarrhea

When you're riding in a Chevy and you're feeling somewhat
heavy... Diarrhea, diarrhea!
When you're sitting in a bush and you feel a little whoosh... Diarrhea,
diarrhea!
When you're sitting by a nerd and you've got to take a turd... Diarrhea,
diarrhea!
When you're climbing up a ladder and you feel a little splatter... Diarrhea,
diarrhea!
When you're sliding into first and you feel a little burst... Diarrhea, diarrhea!
When you're sitting by a tard and you gain a little lard... Diarrhea, diarrhea!
When you're sitting in your class and you feel some heavy gas... Diarrhea,
diarrhea!
When you're biking up the canyon and you bury your
companion... Diarrhea, diarrhea!

Twelve-year-old Kristopher Butcher sang this song for Liz Butcher, student collector, in Logan, Utah, in February 1998. His first two verses commonly appear in other children's versions of the song (see Sherman and Weisskopf 62–63), but his last several verses demonstrate creativity. The last verse about "biking up the canyon" fits Utah's rugged landscape very well.

Yankee Doodle

Yankee Doodle went to town a-ridin' on a gopher
Bumped into a garbage can and this is what fell over:
Great green gobs of greasy, grimy gopher guts,
Mutilated monkey meat, chopped up parakeet.
French-fried eyeballs rolling down the street.
Oops, I forgot my spoon!
So they gave me a split-splat, pus-on-top,
Monkey vomit and camel snot,
All wrapped up in birdie poo,
So eat it, [name], it's good for you!
With vitamin C and protein too
And don't forget the doggie doo!

Sara Miller, who learned this song at a day camp near New York City in the mid-1990s, recorded it in the spring of 2007. The song's main purpose is to "gross out" the listener. Usually associated with school or camp food, the "Gopher Guts" song has delighted generations of children. For other versions, see Sherman and Weisskopf (16–23).

CHEERS

Gigalo

All: Gig ah lo-o, gig gig a lo-o
    Gig ah lo-o, gig gig a lo-o

Group: Hey, Kayla

Kayla: What?

Group: Are you ready to gig?

Kayla: Gig what?

Group: Gigalo

Kayla: My hands up high
    My feet down low
    And this is the way
    I gig a lo [fancy steps or hip-shaking dance]

Group: Her hands up high
    Her feet down low
    And this is the way she gigalos

[repeat from the beginning with the next soloist, and continue until everyone in the group has a turn as soloist]

Azizi Powell, creator of the Cocojams.com Web site, collected this cheer from her daughter, who performed the cheer in Pittsburgh, Pennsylvania, in the mid-1980s. Later, while visiting her daughter and her daughter's students after the turn of the twenty-first century, Powell observed performances of "Gigalo" with the same words as the text she had collected in the 1980s. Like other cheers, this one gives children practice in singing and dancing, both on their own and as members of a group. "Gigalo" has an appealing text and rhythmic sequence. Gaunt's *The Games Black Girls Play* analyzes variants of this cheer (80–85).

Jump in the Car

Jump in the car (clap, clap), step on the gas (clap, clap),
Step back and let (name) pass.
She's got that oo-aah,
Look at that bootie,
Ain't she fine,
If you want it, you've got to pay up on it.

[Children take turns]

Irene Chagall observed one six-year-old and two seven-year-old African American girls playing on their school playground in Marin City, California, in January 2007. After she saw the three girls performing "Jump in the Car" on the playground, she asked them to do it again; they performed the cheer for her without the "bootie" line. During their music class, when the girls recited the cheer again, a male classmate shouted, "Look at that bootie!" (e-mail communication, March 4, 2007).

Chagall comments, "This is not exactly what one wants to have happen during music class, but it sure is a mark of children's folklore." Performances vary according to context. When adults watch and listen, the words may be different from words used when the children are on their own. Male/female interaction also influences performance.

GAMES

Imaginative Games

Playing Store

When I was a little kid we usually played in the sand. We gathered cans and put them on little tables. That's what we call the store.

I always liked to be the store keeper. We used rocks for money and sometimes we stole money from our mother or father. I usually said that a can of pop cost one dollar. The things that we sold were expensive.

Boys pretend to cook leaves in their New York City clubhouse in the late 1970s. Photograph by Martha Cooper.

I made cookies and bread out of mud. Some of my little brothers and sisters ate the mud. I told them not to eat it, but they did.

Cecelia Begaye, a freshman at Intermountain Indian School in Brigham City, Utah, wrote this description for the 1971 school publication *A Look at Me: Writings* (12), kept in the Fife Folklore Archives of Utah State University. One popular role-playing game for young children is playing store, which lets children imitate consumer practices while giving them the chance to make a little money. Cecelia's description shows that it can be fun to make familiar foods out of mud. This is a creative variation on the old custom of making mud pies of dirt, berries, and other materials that are available outdoors.

Keeping House *very gendered*

We didn't play at keeping house on the "mothers and fathers" principle, instead we invented a reason for the father being away. Sometimes he was a lumberjack, sometimes away on business or on holiday. If there happened to be a boy playing with us—which was very rare—he always played father, never mother, but since the woman was in charge at home the father used to be sent out to go shopping or to chaperone the children.

This description of the traditional game of "house" came from a Finnish girl; it was published in Leea Virtanen's *Children's Lore* in 1978 (31). Virtanen suggests that to young players of this game, "The mother represents adult power, a caring but at the same time, tyrannical master" (31). In *Children's Games in Street and Playground,* the Opies make the point that "In domestic dramas the male role is not a popular one; in some young eyes (an East Dulwich 10-year-old's, for example) the father is little more than a figure of fun" (331–32).

Wind Tunnel

In my family's summer cottage the upstairs bedrooms were cooled by a large fan in the hallway. The three of us would take heavy blankets and attach them to the floor to create a wind tunnel. In this wind world we would play with our cars and trucks, but the biggest thing to do was wind talk. To wind talk you put your face right next to the fan and talk into it. When heard from the other side, the voice sounds all distorted and wobbly. This was a really cool thing to do on hot summer days.

Alan, a Scottish American college student from Long Island, recorded his memories of imaginative play with his two brothers in the winter of 1979. In this secluded "wind world," Alan and his brothers created a mode of speech that differed intriguingly from ordinary conversation. Instead of manipulating syllables, as most secret languages do, "wind talk" involved voice distortion. Twenty-three years later, the movie *Windtalkers* (2002) documented Navajo soldiers' use of their native language to create a secret code in World War II.

Charlie's Angels

Three girls each took a name: Sabrina, Kelly, and Chris. Those names correspond with the ever-popular actresses on *Charlie's Angels.* Their mission was to save their friend being held captive by a boy. They did a great deal of running, hiding, and quite a bit of acting which consisted of imitation of the actual actresses in the television show. It was all very exciting to watch. The interesting part of the game was that it didn't seem to end, rather it seemed as though a new episode would be played each day. The friend was finally rescued, and all the children began to scream "yeah" for the three heroines.

Melinda Ames, a student fieldworker, recorded these observations of three 12-year-old girls playing their favorite game in a park in Binghamton, New York, in the spring of 1979. By the late 1970s, imaginative role-playing games based on TV shows had become common. Significantly, the three girls who played the roles of Sabrina, Kelly, and Chris did not take directions from an invisible man named Charlie, as the three actresses did in the original TV show. Exercising their own power of choice, the girls dispensed with the male direction that did not appeal to them: a small but important change.

Hippie and the Cop

Lisa: I know a game we play together. We call it "Hippie and the Cop." I'm the hippie.

Bobby: Guess who I am? (sarcastic intonation). Here, let me tell you the rules. Since I'm the cop, I beat up Lisa with this plastic tubing. If she tries to fight back, I beat her up some more. Then I throw her in jail, a dark room in our cellar. Lisa gets away and then we start all over again. Throughout the game I call her names like "long-haired hippie freak," "pinko turkey," and things like that.

Nine-year-old Lisa and her 11-year-old brother Bobby explained how they played this game in Massapequa, New York, in the spring of 1979. While "Hippie and the Cop" demonstrates creative role-play, it also shows the influence of police dramas on television. Using materials that they could find easily, Lisa and Bobby acted out conflict that was typical of a sensation-oriented TV show. Bobby's verbal abuse of the hippie dramatizes mainstream society's criticism of countercultural lifestyles in the late 1960s and 1970s.

Finger Game

This Is Fred

This is Fred. He says "hi,"
This is Fred when the car goes by.
Each finger tip of right hand has a letter "T" "H" "I" "S"
All four fingers are up for "this"; just "I" and "S" for "is" just "H"
and "I" for "hi." Fred is drawn on the back of right hand, so the hand is
turned so "Fred" can be seen. A car is drawn on the back of left hand.
Left hand slides over right "when the car goes by" (and runs Fred down).

Irene Chagall collected this finger game from an eight-year-old girl in Mill Valley, California, in 2006. The game is quick and easy to play, but it requires careful preparation of the player's hand. Unlike routines of victimization, it puts no one on the spot and simply demonstrates a clever combination of fingers and letters.

Chalk Diagram Games

Skelly

We played on a sidewalk. Sidewalk squares were used as a board. We numbered the board with a piece of chalk. The numbers were placed around the board. There were only four corners. The numbers went from one to eight, beginning in the upper right-hand corner.

A game of Skelly in New York City in the late 1970s. Photograph by Martha Cooper.

Boy looks through a Skelly cap he made from the top of a beer bottle in New York City in the late 1970s. Photograph by Martha Cooper.

The number two lies in the corner diagonally across from one. Then three and four follow this pattern beginning in the upper left-hand corner. Five, six, seven, eight are placed on the sides. Five and six go from top to bottom and seven and eight go side by side starting from left to right.

The game may be played with checkers, but very often it was played with bottle caps. Bottle caps work better because they slide easily in the street, and because they are easier to come by. Bottle caps are basically free, and can be found in abundance.

The game is played so that you flick the bottle cap to number one first. Then the next player tries to flick his bottle cap to number one. Often the first player's bottle cap is pushed out of the first box. The object is to get your bottle cap through each number in order, and the series must be completed to win. If your bottle cap gets knocked out you must begin again.

Rachel, age 44, described this game's rules in Freehold, New Jersey, in April 1981. Rachel played Skelly in the streets of Brooklyn during the 1940s and early 1950s. She had learned that in an earlier version of the game played in the 1920s, hitting the "dead man zone" in the center of the board meant the player had to go back to the beginning of the game. Amanda Dargan and Steven Zeitlin trace this game back to the beginning of the twentieth century and identify variant names, including Skully, Kilsies, Loadsies, and Dead Man (81). Other variants are described in Knapp and Knapp (141–43) and Bronner (187–89).

Aeroplane Hoppy

The taw, a piece of wood, is thrown by the first player into number one base. If it does not go on the line you have a blind man's throw. Then you hop into number two and in and out of the squares until you reach number eight. Then turn around and hop back to number two, pick up your taw, hop over number one and out. Then throw your taw into number two, hop into number three and in and out of the squares until you reach number eight; then back to number three, pick up your taw and hop out.

Next throw your taw into number three, etc., and keep going until you get to number eight. Then you can choose a base and put your name on it (or your initials). Your base is your rest place and no other player is allowed to put a foot in into it. One girl finally wins. Girls from eight to 12 years old play this the year around in the schoolyard.

Dorothy Howard, pioneering collector of Australian children's folklore, collected this description of Hoppy (also known as Hopscotch) from 13-year-old Gwennyth in Swansea in January 1955. Howard suggests that this pattern, which includes two horizontal rows of two squares each, "resembles the two-winged airplane of World War I and probably acquired the name because of the similarity as seen by both Australian and American children" (Darian-Smith and Factor 68–69). Her inclusion of four different versions of Aeroplane Hoppy, as well as many other patterns for the game, demonstrates the richness and diversity of children's folklore. Many other variants of this game can be found in Gomme (1: 223–27), Newell (188–89), and Bronner (189–98).

Running and Chasing Games

Children, Children

All the "children" line up before "mama." At the end, all run and "mama" tries to catch and beat them.

> Children! Children!
> Yes, mama.
> Where have you been to?
> Grandmama.
> What have she given you?
> Bread and cheese.
> Where's my share?
> Up in the air.
> How shall I reach it?
> Climb on a broken chair.
> Suppose I fall?
> I don't care.
> Who learn you such manners?
> Dog.
> Who is the dog?
> You, mama.

Martha Warren Beckwith collected this chasing game in Jamaica between 1919 and 1924; it appears in her 1928 study *Jamaica Folk-Lore* (19). Beckwith notes that like many other games that were popular in Jamaica during that era, this one relies on traditional dialogue from England and Scotland (Gomme 1: 396–98; Newell 143–45). By 1928, many Jamaican young people preferred sports and dance steps to some of the older dialogue-based games, but such games were still part of Jamaican play traditions (Beckwith 5).

Puerto-Rican Tag

It's called Puerto-Rican Tag, and it's like Hide and Go Seek and it's like Leapfrog, and it's really neat. And then you see first, you know, first the person turns around and covers their eyes and counts to about fifty, or whatever the chosen number is. And *then,* everybody hides, and if the person, once the person is three feet or five feet away…they're supposed to run out in front of 'em. Now to defend yourself is to go under to bend down over and if the person bends over, the person has to *leapfrog* over 'em. And after about three people have been leapfrogged, or something like that, you know…everybody races back and the one who's left there is it. But the thing is, if you're tagged when you're ducked down, you're automatically it.

Eleven-year-old Barbara explained this game to me in Bloomington, Indiana, in March 1977 ("Tradition and Creativity" 537). Her excitement about playing three games at once shines through in her description. Both Leapfrog and Hide-and-Seek involve vigorous movement. Tag, which has taken many forms, is one of the most variable and entertaining games known to elementary-school children.

Ringalevio

Everyone could play. What you do is choose up sides. It does not make a difference how many people you've got. You can have four on each side, five on each side. The game is best with three or more.

One side stays in a designated area and counts to one hundred while the other side hides. After the side that is "it" counts to one hundred, they begin looking for the other side. If a person who has been hiding is found, you bring them to an area which acts like a pen. Now anyone who is still in hiding can come in and free these guys in the pen. All he has to do is yell "Ringalevio" and then everyone in the team is freed from the pen and may hide again.

Nick, a 67-year-old Russian American who played Ringalevio in Brooklyn in the 1920s, described the game's rules in Freehold, New Jersey, in April 1981. Alice Bertha Gomme includes a variant called Relievo in the second volume of her *Traditional Games* (107); Simon J. Bronner describes a game called Rolevo in his study of American children's games (184). Since this game involves team formation, it represents a higher level of organization than central-person games such as Tag.

Pirañas

It's called Pirañas and somebody is a piraña, and you have as many people as you want. And they swim around, and if the piraña comes up and bites you on the foot or on the arm, you have to sink and touch the bottom before you can come back up. And the piraña has to make sure you do.

Amanda, age eight, described this game in Binghamton, New York, in April 1987. Less well known than the popular swimming pool chasing game Marco Polo (Knapp and Knapp 52; Bronner 179), this one lets children imitate pursuit of prey by carnivorous fish.

Ball Games

Spud

One player is chosen to be "it." A ball is tossed into the air while the other players try to run as far away as possible. When "it" catches the ball, he immediately yells "Spud" and all the other players must freeze. "It" then takes three steps toward any player, throws the ball and attempts to hit one player. If "it" hits another player with the ball, the player receives the letter S. This continues until one player gets the entire word "Spud." The first player to spell out the word becomes the new "it."

Deborah Haines wrote this description of Spud in Gary, Indiana, in 1972; Gary Hall included it in his "Folkgames" essay in 1973 (73). Like various Tag games, Spud involves role reversal and energetic running. This version, like the basketball games of Pig or Horse, lets players accumulate letters that delay the moment of losing until the word becomes complete.

Stoopball

You play against cement stairs with a Pensy Pinky. Anybody can play and everyone plays against everybody else. Throw the ball at the stairs and try to catch it after it bounces back. If the ball bounces more than twice you lose your turn and the next player is up. The scoring goes: catch it on a fly, it's ten points; catch it in one bounce, it's five; and if the ball bounces off the edge of the stoop, 'cause it's hard to catch and comes off the stoop fast, it's worth fifty points. Whoever gets five hundred points first wins.

Aaron, 11 years old, described Stoopball in Flushing, New York, in April 1979. This typical New York street game involves simple materials: an inexpensive pink rubber ball and a concrete stoop. Common from the 1940s to the 1980s, Stoopball is played less often now (Dargan and Zeitlin 50–54; Knapp and Knapp 141; Bronner 187). Web surfers can find the game's rules on http://www.streetplay.com.

Butt Ball

All the players line up in front of a wall and use smaller balls (usually tennis balls) that they throw against the wall. If they do not catch it after the first bounce they then have to run and touch the wall before being hit in the butt by a ball being thrown by another player. If they do not make it, they are out until the next round but if they do make it they get a chance to throw it and try to hit someone else until there are only 2–3 players left.

While student teaching at Wellsville Elementary School in Utah in April 1998, Melissa Williams recorded her observation of this popular game. Williams noted that although Utah children had enjoyed playing Butt Ball since the 1980s, playground supervisors discouraged children from playing it. This is one of many variants of Wall Ball, including Suicide, discussed in chapter 4.

Snowballs

A couple of my friends and I made up a game to play in the winter, when it snowed. We would build a snow fort down towards the end of the yard, that blocked us from the road. When a car would drive by, we would throw snowballs at the back of their car. Where

Boys play ball in Innsbruck, Austria, in the summer of 1992. Photograph by Geoffrey Gould.

the snowball hit would determine how many points you got. I don't remember the exact points now, but the most was for hitting the back window, and you would get no points if you missed the car. The only problem was that occasionally people would stop their cars and yell at us.

Paul, an Anglo-American college student from Albany, New York, described this winter game in November 2000. Although Paul and his friends invented the game, they used the familiar pattern of giving points for hits, as in Stoopball and other neighborhood ball games. This game's subversive quality makes it a childhood underground game, usually not divulged to parents or teachers.

Boy/Girl Games

Choo-Choo

The leader starts by marching and saying "Choo-choo." He taps a person on the shoulder and they put their arms around the leader's back and enter another room. The leader then kisses the person he picked. Another person is picked, and so on. A train is the end result. As each person is being picked, each member of the train kisses the person behind them. When only one person is left, they have the idea of the game. Except when it comes to his turn to be kissed, the last person receives a light slap on the face instead. Obviously, the joke is on him.

Marilyn, age 13, explained how to play this game during a birthday party for her 12-year-old friend in New York City in April 1979. Choo-Choo is well established in American folk tradition. Brian Sutton-Smith identifies it as a popular pursuit in his 1959 essay "The Kissing Games of Adolescents in Ohio" (470–71); Mary and Herbert Knapp also describe it in *One Potato, Two Potato* (218). Sutton-Smith observes that it is customary for players of Choo-Choo, sometimes called Pony Express, to give the last child who joins the train a playful slap. He also notes this game's similarity to Fox and Goose in Gomme's *Traditional Games of England, Scotland, and Ireland* (1: 139).

Truth or Dare

Jackie: Did you ever feel it? A boy's, I mean.

Colleen: (blushes) Give me a dare.

Paula: Okay, then you see that man over there? (points) You have to go over to him and kiss him and then you come back here.

Colleen: (walks toward man and returns without completing her dare) I can't do that. Okay, I'll tell you guys that I didn't ever touch it and I don't want to. Not yet anyway.

Jackie, Colleen, and Paula, all 12 years old, played Truth or Dare in a New York City park in April 1979. Initially they stood in a circle, lit a cigarette, and passed the cigarette around so that each girl could inhale. Whoever took a drag from the cigarette while ashes fell to the ground had to answer a personal question truthfully or perform a dare.

Mary and Herbert Knapp include Truth or Dare in their discussion of children's kissing games; a typical dare is "Kiss Esther on the ear" (217). It is, of course, harder to kiss a stranger than to kiss a classmate or acquaintance, so Colleen's decision to tell the truth instead of completing her dare makes good sense. Few folklorists have studied this kind of game playing, which usually takes place in a secluded setting.

Spin the Bottle

Well, I have gone to lots of parties where everybody plays this game, but I don't like to play. I'm kind of going out with Jerry and he's in the seventh grade, so he wouldn't be at the parties. Anyway, you have to get a Coke bottle that *must* be from the party. Then you sit in a circle or else near each other in a group. One person takes the bottle and spins it.

Wherever it lands, you have to kiss that person. Usually if it is someone you don't like, you sort of stall, hoping everyone won't make you kiss them. But most of the time you have to kiss because they make you.

Thirteen-year-old Maureen told her older sister, Melissa, about playing Spin the Bottle in Mahopac, New York, in April 1987. At first, Maureen hesitated to talk about the game. After Melissa explained that she had played Spin the Bottle too, Maureen felt better about describing her own experience. Their family heritage was Irish American.

In his survey of Ohio children's and college students' kissing games in 1959, Brian Sutton-Smith found that Spin the Bottle was the most popular game. He observes that children often cheat so that they can kiss the person of their choice (467–80). Mary and Herbert Knapp note that games of this kind "excuse a child from selecting a partner (a most onerous task for younger children) and eliminate the possibility of being deliberately left out" (219). Perhaps this inclusivity explains why Spin the Bottle is still played in the United States in the early twenty-first century.

Pass the Card

Take a card of some kind, maybe an ID or a credit card—but kids don't have credit cards. Hold the card in your mouth with suction and then pass it to the next person, to their mouth, and they have to use suction to hold it. The game goes guy/girl, guy/girl. The point of the game is not to drop the card, but if someone drops it, he has to kiss the person he drops it with. The whole point is to kiss somebody.

Robert, a 22-year-old college student of Anglo-American descent, explained this game's rules to me in Vestal, New York, in August 2007. He had watched middle-school friends play the game between 1998 and 2000.

Although the use of a plastic ID card gives this kissing game a contemporary flair, the game is quite old. In *Games and Songs of American Children*, William Wells Newell identifies a game in which a button or whisper is passed around a circle (151). Brian Sutton-Smith lists three versions of the game in "Kissing Games of Adolescents in Ohio": Pass the Kiss, Pass the Lifesaver, and Pass the Orange (476). Late twentieth-century and early twenty-first-century variants of this game include passing compact discs and straws from mouth to mouth. The "guy/girl, guy/girl" lineup ensures that some interesting kisses or near-kisses will take place.

Dangerous Games

Lying Down in the Street

When I was eight years old, I belonged to a group of friends on a Navy base in Yokohama, Japan, that enjoyed experimenting with danger. We had baby aspirin-eating contests and high-speed bike races. Our most exciting game was called "lying down in the street." We would take turns lying down on one of our neighborhood's streets and watching for cars, calculating the precise moment when it would be safe to jump up and run to safety. All of us took pride in jumping up in time. I never considered how alarming this game would be for the drivers.

This is my own recollection of learning to play a game that folklorists have documented since the early 1900s (Douglas 80; Opie and Opie, *Children's Games* 269–72; Hall 75). Now, as a parent and teacher, I worry about such games—but then I felt sure I could stay safe by watching for cars and running fast.

Railroad Chicken

To play Railroad Chicken you put your head on the rail and at the last possible moment as a train approaches, you roll down the embankment. Part of the thrill comes from being so close to the passing train, you can feel it trying to trying to suck you in. It's not played very often because it's too long between trains.

Eddie Bullard explained the rules of this game played in Haw River, North Carolina, to Gary Hall in 1972; his description became part of Hall's "Folkgames" essay (75). Railroad Chicken offers a combination of fear and excitement, as the fast-moving train offers the possibility of death or serious injury. Highly subversive and dangerous, this game has appealed to some adolescents who want to prove their courage.

Hangman

Did you ever play Hangman in real life? It's very dangerous. What we do is, we don't use letters or nothing. We take a rope, and it gots a hole in it, and you put it around their head. We close it as tight as we can and see who can choke himself the longest.

Nine-year-old Derek described his involvement in Hangman in Binghamton, New York, in May 1987. Members of the childhood underground have tried to keep adults from learning about this extremely dangerous game. Some of the game's nicknames include Funky Chicken, Rocket Ride, Rising Sun, and California Choke. Warnings from sheriffs and other experts in children's safety now appear on the Internet.

PRANKS

Seeing Stars in the Daytime

"Seeing stars in the daytime" was popular years ago among Oconto County children. A visitor or new resident in the neighborhood would be asked if he or she would like to see stars in the daytime. The answer was, usually, "yes." He would be taken to the woodshed or down in the cellar or other dark place, and the armhole of a coat sleeve would be fitted over his face. He would then be asked, "Do you see the stars yet?" The answer would be "no." "Then close your eyes and open them real quick." At that, a dip of cold water would descend into the blinking eyes to the utter discomfort of the victim who wouldn't rest until he found someone who "wanted to see the stars"; (I know because I was initiated when I was ten!)

Mrs. Morton H. Starr described this clever prank in her essay "Wisconsin Pastimes" (1954). With a few simple props, these children taught each other not to be gullible. Once they had rubbed the water out of their eyes, the children hastened to put others through similar discomfort.

"Please Don't Answer Your Phone"

Here's one that's really funny. We call and say, "Hello, we're the electric company. We are fixing the lines now, so please don't answer your phone if it rings in the next hour. If you answer the phone, the calling party will immediately be electrocuted." So about twenty minutes later, we dial and when the person picks up, we scream on our end.

Fourteen-year-old Earl described his favorite prank in Bethpage, New York, in March 1983. This classic telephone prank gives the prankster a feeling of power (Knapp and Knapp 100–101). Although the prevalence of caller ID has made such pranks more risky, the tradition of prank calling continues.

Wedgies and Pink Bellies

We would give rookie treatment to all the new Scouts, like wedgies and pink bellies. We gave wedgies until their underwear was all the way up their crotch or until their underpants ripped. If they didn't rip, we hanged them on hooks and watched them dangle. The pink bellies are a classic. We slapped their stomachs until they were rosy red and if they were really bad, we would use toothpaste—Crest mint flavor was the worst. It stung like hell.

John, a 20-year-old resident of Long Island, New York, enjoyed reminiscing about Boy Scout camp pranks in May 1981. These two fit Sheldon Posen's category of sexual pranks; they also resemble initiatory hazing for new soldiers. Wedgies, common both at camp and at school, rudely show who can torment whom; Pink Bellies fulfill the same function.

Snipe Hunt

The first time I heard of snipes, I was on a hayride, and this guy we were with says, "Let's go on a snipe hunt!" I said, "A snipe hunt? What's a snipe hunt?" He says, "Don't worry—let's just go." So we went into the woods and he said, "Start looking for snipes." So we all started looking for snipes, not knowing what we were looking for, just beating the bushes, and just looking. Then finally, I just got real tired and frustrated, because I couldn't find a snipe, because I didn't know what a snipe was—I was getting frustrated looking for something I didn't know. After I realized we'd been fooled, I started laughing at the people still looking. So that was my first encounter with snipes.

David Chinery collected this narrative from a female senior at Cook College in New Brunswick, New Jersey, and published the text in his "Snooping for Snipes" (1987). This classic prank has been traced back to lumberjacks' and hunters' initiatory behavior in northern Wisconsin during the first half of the twentieth century (Starr 184). Snipes, elusive shorebirds, do exist, but not in wooded areas. For another good example of a snipe hunt, see Bronner (170–71).

Switching Places

Kim and I would switch places in school. We did this a lot in the fourth grade. When we came into class I would go to her seat and she would go to mine. The teacher would never notice, ever. The only problem we had was when we had writing assignments. I write with my right hand and she writes with her left hand. So both of us would have to switch our writing hands, and that never worked.

Diane Lutes told student fieldworker Judith Rush about switching places with her twin sister Diane in Hummelstown, Pennsylvania, in 1986. Her story is one of many amusing anecdotes in Rush's "Twin Pranks and Practical Jokes" (1987). Rush concludes that twin pranks let twins "perform for their peers" and "retaliate at a society who sees them as a unit" (6). It is not surprising to hear that identical twins have the best success in playing such pranks, while fraternal twins have a lower success rate.

Live Chickens and Grasshoppers

Back in high school, I decided I wanted to do a senior prank right before the last day of school with a friend. I brought two live chickens with my friend Mike and numbered one of the chickens one and one of them three. I also brought a bunch of grasshoppers for my prank. So a few days before our last day of school, I drove to school with Mike and told him to wait in the car until I called him. I went into school through the front doors and walked around the school checking which exit was free to let Mike through. This was all near lunchtime, so it was easier to find an exit to sneak someone in.

As soon as I found an exit near the back of the school, I called Mike right away. He came within a few minutes with a box holding the chickens and a bag with the grasshoppers. We quickly snuck up to the third floor and released our chickens. After a few seconds, we started hearing shrieks through the hallway because some people were in the hallway. We released the grasshoppers through a little crack in the door and we quietly snuck away. Two of the deans caught the chickens, and I haven't found out what happened to the grasshoppers. We luckily got away with our prank without getting caught in the end.

Anthony, 19 years old, whose family heritage was Hispanic, told the story of his favorite high school prank in Vestal, New York, in April 2007. This gleeful story shows how much fun it can be to transform an orderly high school into a chaotic animal playground. Such transformations, which symbolize students' subversive spirit, have also been popular on college campuses. For examples of comparable college pranks, see my 2005 study *Campus Legends* (41–42).

NARRATIVES

Tales

Boo!

There was once a girl who was home alone because her mother and father were at a party. At seven o'clock a voice said, "At eleven o'clock you must go up to the attic and open the old trunk. If you don't you will be killed." It was ten o'clock, ten thirty, and finally eleven. The girl shook as she went up the stairs at eleven o'clock. She opened the trunk and there was a voice which said: "BOO!"

Reimund Kvideland includes this story collected from a 12-year-old boy in Bergen, Norway, in 1969 in his essay "Stories about Death as a Part of Children's Socialization" (62). Kvideland persuasively argues that stories help children learn about the meaning of death in an entertaining, nonthreatening way. Such stories often include spooky sounds that frighten a child (Motif E402, "Mysterious ghostlike noises heard"). Children have continued to enjoy stories of this kind from the 1970s to the early twenty-first century. Other examples are included in Sylvia Grider's "Supernatural Narratives of Children" (211–38) and my "Tradition and Creativity in the Storytelling of Pre-Adolescent Girls" (121–41).

One Black Eye

One night, see there's this...a mother, a father, a little boy, a little girl, and a baby. And they went downtown and the little baby says, "Give me a lollipop." So he got a lollipop. So the next night, they went home. And the next morning everybody got up. No...just the father got up and the mother said, "Go down and get some milk." And he went down there an the ghost came out an he says, "One black eye." And the father runs back up and he says, "Oh, there is not." So she runs down and he says, "One black eye." And she jumped up there. She says for the little boy to go down there. And he went down and: "One black eye." And he got the sister and she went down: "One black eye." So she came back up and she told the little baby to go down there. And he had his lollipop with him, a great big ole lollipop. The monster says, "One black eye." The baby says, "You'd better shut up or you're going to have *two* black eyes!"

John M. Vlach collected this tale from 10-year-old Krystal Wood at her elementary school in Spencer, Indiana, in October 1971; it was published in his article "One Black Eye and Other Horrors: A Case for the Humorous Anti-Legend" and deposited in the Indiana University Archives (72–82-F).

In his analysis of this tale and others, Vlach emphasizes the importance of "at least a token belief" for the punch line to make people laugh (122). "One Black Eye" releases tension related to scary noises and gives the youngest child the honor of defeating the ghost with a verbal putdown. A 2001 version in the form of a joke appears in Sara Staunton's "Riddle Use" (99); another variant can be found in Bronner (156).

Johnny, I'm on the First Step

There was this little boy and his mother told him to get some liver. So the mother gave him some money and he bought candy and forgot about the liver. So he stabbed a man and took out his liver. He brought it home and his mother made it for dinner.

So that night, when the mother and father went out, the dead man came to get his liver back. Well, Johnny was sleeping when he heard "Johnny, I'm by the door." But Johnny just went back to sleep. And then Johnny heard "Johnny, I'm on the first step, Johnny, I'm near your mother's room, I'm near your door. Johnny, I'm in your room." And then he stabbed the boy.

Sally, a second-grader, told this tale in her classroom in Brooklyn, New York, in March 1979. This "gross-out" story has delighted many children. Based on Aarne-Thompson tale type 366, "The Man from the Gallows," the story shows how dangerous it can be to show disrespect for the dead. In most versions of this story, Johnny does not kill anyone to get a liver; instead, he gets a dead person's liver in a cemetery (Tucker, "Tradition and Creativity" 131–32, 495–96; Grider, 198–201; Bronner 158). In Sally's story, Johnny's stabbing of a man results in his getting stabbed by the man's ghost: just punishment for a serious crime.

Legends

Cosmic Candy

Todd: A long, long time ago, one of the kids from *Eight is Enough,* the little kid—

Collector: You mean Nicholas?

Todd: Yeah, well the little kid, he ate five packs of Cosmic Candy and lots of soda and he blew up.

Nate: And all the other people on the show ate him.

Todd: They did not! He just blew up.

Collector: Was this on TV or in real life?

Todd: No, it really happened. It was on the news and you heard the boom and everything.

When Mindy Jackson, a student at Binghamton University, was giving a barbecue in her backyard in Johnson City, New York, in the spring of 1980, seven-year-old Todd and five-year-old Nate came over to tell a few stories, which Mindy recorded. Around this time period, as Gary Alan Fine's 1979 study "Folklore Diffusion through Interactive Social Networks" shows, legends about carbon-dioxide-filled candy exploding in children's stomachs were circulating actively. This exchange between Todd and his younger brother Nate is a good example of legend dialectics: a claim that might or might not be true, followed by doubt and then insistence that the story is true.

Mary Whales

Well, they say that Mary Whales was going to a party one night; and after the parties she asked her boyfriend to take her home; and he didn't want to go home right then and they got into an argument. And so she was walking home that night in the rain and she crossed the street and got hit by a car and was killed. And they say that every time that it rains that she stands on the corner of 38th and Northwestern and hitchhikes a ride and if you don't give her a ride you will crash at the next stop light. And if you do give her a ride she will tell you to take her to a big white house and by the time that you get there she will be gone and the back seat of the car will be wet.

And another way that I hear it is that she went to a party and she ask her boyfriend to drop her off at the drugstore and so he did. And she was walking home in the rain and she got hit by a car and she died in the hospital and she was buried two days later. And ever since then when it rains she stands on the corner of 38th and Northwestern and hitches a ride. And it has the same ending as the other one.

Thirteen-year-old Debra gave these two variants of the legend of Mary Whales to Janet L. Langlois on a questionnaire at Holy Angels Elementary School in Indianapolis, Indiana, on February 8, 1973. Langlois published Debra's stories in her 1978 essay "'Mary Whales, I Believe in You': Myth and Ritual Subdued" (18–19).

These two legend variants add substance to the ritual of summoning Mary Whales, Mary Worth, or Bloody Mary, which involves repeating Mary's name a certain number of times while standing in front of a mirror in a darkened bathroom or other room. The legends, which follow the well-established pattern of the "Vanishing Hitchhiker" cycle, provide details about Mary's sudden death, which may explain her desire to hurt those who dare to summon her.

In "'Mary Whales, I Believe in You,'" Langlois analyzes the relationship between legend and game in relation to myth and ritual. Alan Dundes's "Bloody Mary in the Mirror" (2002) applies psychoanalytic theory to this widespread phenomenon of the childhood underground.

Potato Chips and Milk

There was this girl once who was going babysitting at a new house for the first time. When she got there it was afternoon and the people weren't going to be home until midnight. They left her nothing to eat, and the T.V. was broken. Before they left, they told her she could do anything she wanted except for opening the closet door.

As it got later and later she got hungrier and hungrier, and she kept wondering what was in the closet. Finally she couldn't stand it any more and she opened the door. Inside was lots and lots of potato chips and big glasses of milk. She ate them all up. When the people got home she was dead on the floor. Do you know why? They weren't potato chips and milk, they were scabs and pus.

Eleven-year-old Sally told this story at her home in Suffield, Connecticut, in October 1977. This is one of many legends about beleaguered babysitters, which were very popular in the 1960s and 1970s (see Bronner 151–52). This babysitting situation bodes no good: miserly parents leave no food and a broken TV. Here we recognize the "Bluebeard" tale pattern: a forbidden room or door, the opening of which will lead to punishment. The babysitter dies from contamination; what she thought was a tasty snack was actually disgusting by-products of infection. I heard a variant of the "Potato Chips" story as an 11-year-old in Washington, D.C., in 1959.

The China Doll

This one woman loves to buy china dolls, and since her husband is rich she likes to buy the best ones. One day she goes up to the finest store in America for china dolls. She finds a beautiful one in the store. The cost is over $4,000, but she doesn't care, she loves it. The artwork was hand-painted, but she notices something. The doll has teeth. Wondering—well, she says she doesn't care. When she hands the money to the owner he says, "You don't want that, lady! That thing is haunted." Haunted? What kind of nut was this? She knew then that she was going to write a complaint to the owner of the store. She said, "Just put it in the bag, mister." That was what she said. She paid the bill.

She comes home. She puts it in her big collection where all the other dolls are. But this time she puts it on the top shelf. Laughing. "Haunted!" She goes to bed. In the middle of the night she hears "Scratch, scratch, scratch." She thinks it's just her dream and goes back to sleep.

In the morning she wakes up before her husband. She goes up to feed the canary and all of a sudden she sees it dead. Clawed to death. Stricken, she screams a loud shriek. Her husband comes and finds what happened. When she sees the doll, she finds his nails have grown longer and he has blood that resembles the canary. She doesn't know what to do and neither does her husband. She buries the canary in a shoe box, giving it a fitting ending, and thinks what must have happened: the canary got loose and who knows, maybe the cat got it.

The next day she hears the same noise, "scratch, scratch." She thinks, "Oh, no, not the cat again!" She goes back to sleep. In the morning she finds her cat dead. Mauled to death like the canary. She goes to see if there was a vandal who did something to her dolls, then she sees the dolls. Their finger nails have grown longer and they have the blood which looks like the cat's. Then she screams, but the voice doesn't come out of her lips. She's scared to say a word. Maybe that sales clerk wasn't dumb after all. Who knows. Couldn't have been true. She gets scared again. She doesn't know what to do. She just goes back to sleep til the end of the night. She hears a scratch, but it's louder and louder. She goes back to sleep. In the morning she finds her husband mauled and scratched terribly over the chest. He lies there dead, sheets soaked and stained with blood.

Reporting this to the police, she gets scared. She thinks about the china doll and the nails and runs back. This time the nails are bigger and he has the blood of her husband. She screams and picks up the doll and throws it outside in the garbage can. For protection she takes a baseball bat, that's her son's who's away at college, and sleeps with it. In the middle of the night she hears "scratch, scratch," a sound of scraping of metal. She hears another distant scratch, but doesn't know what it is. Then she hears one close; soon she can see little holes begin in her door. She picks up the baseball bat and sees the doll walking in. The doll with the nails pointing right at her. She begins to hit the doll with the bat, banging and banging it, shattering the doll to a hundred little pieces. The doll died, of course, in a way. So what she does is she scoops it up. She takes it back to the sales clerk. She tells him the story. He believed it. He said it happened to three other people. He picks up the charred remains and begins to glue them up. And another woman then buys it. Then she begins to hear the scratching noise. And again the story continues.

This extraordinarily detailed story came from Elliott, a fifth-grader at a private school for Jewish students in upstate New York, in May 1987. Elliott's talent in developing complex episodes and using strategically placed sound effects makes this a fine example of the "China Doll" narrative, which has circulated in oral tradition since the mid-twentieth century (and probably earlier). In many variants of this legend, a seafaring father buys a doll for his daughter in China and sends the doll home to her; then the doll kills each member of the family, one by one.

The last part of Elliott's story resembles what happens at the end of "Johnny, I'm on the first step" stories. Although we might expect the doll to kill the woman, it does not, and the woman successfully returns the doll to the store where she bought it. Why does the store owner glue the doll together to sell it to someone else? This macabre ending makes the story even more sinister than it would otherwise seem.

Ralph and Rudy

They [Ralph and Rudy] were brothers and they worked as hired hands on the farm. And they both were really hard workers and really good people to have around, but they were like day and night. Ralph was an alcoholic, he drank a lot, went on benders and came home, and every time they'd come home they'd have a big fight. Besides, when Ralph wasn't on one of his drunks, they worked real hard and they would bring vegetables and stuff up from the yard.

One time Ralph was out on one of his drunks and he came home all drunked up and Rudy was waiting for him. And—which usually happened—they'd get in a big fight, every time he comes home they get in a big fight. So they got in a *real* big fight. And they really tore up the house, rolled out into the yard, and in the yard they—they were farmers and you know if you're a farmer or any kind of a skilled craftsman or anything you keep your tools in excellent condition. It's something that—you know you just don't—like *our* houses [at the camp], you don't have anything in it that isn't as sharp as it should be or anything. But these guys really kept their tools—they sharpened their shovels and took really good care of things.

So they roll out in the yard and in the yard was a chopping block, and in it was a double-edged axe. OK, and they rolled around and they were fighting and Ralph picked up the axe and tried to swing it at Rudy but it slipped out of his hands and flew out into the yard. So they're really, *really* fighting, it's a good fight, they're really hitting each other and there's a lot of cuts and bruises and they're rolling around. But the story takes a turn for the worse now because they roll near the double-edged axe. And Ralph picks up the axe and swings it and cuts Rudy's head off at the neck with just one big swipe 'cause it's so sharp.

Now you know what happens, like the two veins going up your neck that carries all the blood about every minute or two to your head and back to your body? So when that is severed all of a sudden like that, the heart keeps pumping, it keeps pumping it out like a fire hose. Well, this stuff pumped out and hit Ralph right in the face, through Rudy's head, just really splattered his face.

This part of the legend "Ralph and Rudy" was narrated by camp counselor Bill Henry at Longview Riding Camp near Georgetown, Kentucky, during the summer of 1972. The legend continued to be told at Hiram House Camp near Cleveland, Ohio, from 1973 to 1978. Bill Ellis published his transcription of Henry's legend in "'Ralph and Rudy': The Audience's Role in Re-creating a Camp Legend" (173–74).

Ellis explains that the key narrators of camp legends are adult counselors who shape the stories through interaction with their campers. He notes that "Ralph and Rudy" fits the pattern of the "Dismembered Hermit" legend often told at children's camps. This legend has three parts: an explanation of how Rudy turned into a maniac, a confrontation between Rudy and the camp owner's wife, and a warning to campers.

The Counselor's Death

There was once a jail about a hundred miles from Surprise Lake Camp. One summer night when camp was in session there was a prison break, and one of the prisoners got away. He was notorious for axing women to death, raping and axing them to death. The night that this guy broke out of jail it was raining, it was cold, damp and rainy, one of those real dark, gloomy nights. They put out an all points bulletin and everyone was searching the area for this guy. Especially all the girls had to beware, because they knew he was heading in the direction of the camp and they wanted everybody to be safe.

These two counselors that lived together, girl counselors, one of them went to bed about 10:00 because she wasn't feeling very well. She assumed that the other counselor would come in; she was supposed to put the eight little girls to sleep and then come to bed. So she went to sleep and about 2:00 in the morning she heard steps coming up. It was real dark in her room, and they didn't have lights because the electricity went out because of the storm. She assumed that the other counselor she was living with came in and was asleep. She heard this gnawing sound on the door, and she got really scared because she thought this man was going to come and rape her and kill her. She pretended not to hear, she hid her head under the pillows and tried to go to sleep and this sound continued, and then eventually it stopped. She wasn't feeling very well, so she fell back asleep.

When she got up in the morning, she opened the door. Her other counselor was on the other side of the door dead, with a hatchet in the back of her head. The sound that she had heard was that girl's fingernails trying to scratch on the door to get her to open it. They never found the guy who escaped from prison, and he's looming somewhere around, so beware!

Nineteen-year-old Erica narrated this legend in Vestal, New York, in November 1978. Erica had learned the story at Surprise Lake Camp in Cold Spring, New York, 10 years earlier.

This horror legend combines plot elements from the well-known legends "The Hook," "The Hatchet Man," and "The Roommate's Death." Most versions of "The Roommate's Death" take place on a college campus; after hearing scratches on the door of her residence hall room, a female student finds her roommate lying outside the door with a knife in her back. This legend, which emphasizes young women's vulnerability to danger, has been analyzed by a number of folklorists, including Linda Dégh, author of "The Roommate's Death and Other Related Dormitory Stories in Formation." We can guess that the story of "The Counselor's Death" became part of Surprise Lake Camp's oral tradition when a female counselor who had heard "The Roommate's Death" at college decided to create a new version of the legend to scare young campers.

Cornish

I went to Surprise Lake Camp in Cold Spring, New York, for two years. The biggest ghost story around was about Cornish, a hike trail that we often went on. Cornish was more of a trail than a hike. It had been an estate a long time ago belonging to the Cornish family. When you go up there you see the rundown remains of the property. It was a huge estate, clearly belonging to a very rich family. Some say they raised Cornish hens and that's where Cornish hens got their name, but I'm not sure if that's really true.

The legend goes that a man lived there with his wife and two or three children, and one day he went crazy and killed them all with an axe. There are three notches in a large rock. People say that it took him three tries to kill his wife on that rock, because she kept moving her head, but on the third try he decapitated her.

Now it is tradition for the boys to all pee on that rock when they pass it, otherwise it's bad luck. If you wake up with a red leaf under your pillow the morning after you go past Cornish, it means you're going to die. I don't know of that ever happening to anyone; I don't think anyone has ever died at that camp.

Anyway, the end of that story is that after he killed his family, he burned down his house and just broke down. Some hikers found him a few days later shaking and rocking under a tree, the axe next to him. They brought him to a hospital and he's still living in an insane asylum nearby. I forget the name of it, but my friend told me what it was.

Sam, a 19-year-old alumnus of Surprise Lake Camp, narrated this text in April 2006. His story combines place-name legendry with the well-known horror legend plot sequence of a man going crazy and murdering people with an axe. Studies of camp horror legends of that kind include Lee Haring and Mark Breslerman's "The Cropsey Maniac" (1977) and my "Cropsey at Camp" (2006).

RITUALS

Be Real Quiet

Everybody gets into a big circle that wanta play, and it has to be *real quiet,* and it's really supposed to be dark, but the fire will be okay. And you gotta *concentrate.* And then, after that, everybody's quiet, and then we bring like Frankenstein or Dracula, one of them back. And then we all hold hands and be real quiet.

Linda, an African American fifth-grader, told her fellow Girl Scout troop members how to hold a séance during a campout at the Bradford Woods campsite near Martinsville, Indiana, in October 1976. Her description became part of my dissertation, "Tradition and Creativity in the Storytelling of Pre-Adolescent Girls" (403).

Since the nineteenth century, American children have enjoyed trying to raise the dead by holding séances. While children's séance routines vary, everyone usually sits in a circle holding hands and tries to stay very quiet. Linda uses the word *quiet* three times in her description, showing that nothing interesting will happen unless the group refrains from making noise. Unlike some children who have tried to raise the spirits of dead individuals, she suggests that the group should try to bring back the spirits of monsters in horror films. This choice demonstrates the dominance of mass-media images in American culture during the late twentieth century. For other séance examples, see Bronner (166–67).

Séance at Lizzie Borden's Home

For my thirteenth birthday, my mom took me and three of my friends to go stay at the house of Lizzie Borden, a woman who, at the age of twenty, murdered her entire family in that house. The house is rumored to be haunted by her ghost and the ghosts of her family members. Many people say that these are malevolent ghosts, as many ghosts who suffered violent deaths are.

While I was there, my friends and I had a séance. While we were doing that, all the candles blew out by themselves, and in the one lamp that we had turned on, the light bulb exploded. At one point, I felt hands on my neck and something began to choke me. My friend grabbed a flashlight and turned it on and the choking stopped, but a few times during the night, I felt something pull my hair. The whole experience was really scary, but fun at the same time because I love to be scared.

Irina, a college junior of Russian descent, told this story in Vestal, New York, in November 2003. Her choice of Lizzie Borden's former home as the place to spend the night of her 13th birthday demonstrates the appeal of a "good scare" in a safe setting. The proprietors of Lizzie Borden Bed and Breakfast in Fall River, Massachusetts, have promoted their business through a mystery-oriented Web site that plays the jump-rope rhyme "Lizzie Borden." Since Borden was never proven guilty of her parents' murders, the site of their death remains mysterious.

Every Birthday Morning

Okay, someone has to lay on the floor. Now you rub their temples and say in a scary voice, "Every birthday morning since she can remember, a little girl goes up to her mom's room to check for presents. No one is in the room or the house and it's very dark."

There's a note on a picture that says, "We killed your mom and dad on your birthday and we're coming to get you." The note is written in blood and there's a knife hanging from the picture. She tries to run out of the house but hears footsteps chasing her. The man catches and kills the little girl.

Jerri, age 13, told this story in Garden City, New York, in the spring of 1980. Her story describes a trance session: a storytelling event during which children make each other the central characters in truly frightening scenarios. After the listener lies down on the floor, the storyteller rubs the listener's temples while explaining that the listener has just lost her parents and will soon die a violent death herself. If the listener cries or screams, the storyteller succeeds in her objective.

This story highlights the ritual of receiving birthday presents. Inversion of the expectation of birthday happiness turns the day into a tragedy. Few horror stories could be worse than this one, which seems guaranteed to make the young listener scream or cry. Scholarship on this subject is discussed in chapter 4.

Ouija Board

I was at Becky's house, and we decided to try out her Ouija board. Katie and another girl were also there. Katie and I decided not to take part, so we sat on the couch to watch while Becky and the other girl sat on the floor with the board. They asked if there was a spirit in the room, and the, um, thing that you put your hands on went to yes. I wasn't taking it seriously, and Katie was giggling, so I guess she didn't either. But Becky and the other girl were very nervous, and they didn't know what to ask next.

I suggested they ask "the spirit" what nickname I'd been calling Katie. Since I only used it when we were talking on the phone, nobody else would know it. They asked the spirit, and it began to spell out a name: "W-I-N-S-T-O-N." Winston! That's what I called Katie! I called her Winston because I'd read somewhere that Winston Churchill was famous for saying clever, witty things. Katie was constantly saying stupid things, so I called her Winston as a joke. Anyway, it was really creepy.

Before we had a chance to think of another question, "the spirit" began to talk again. It was spelling out "lamp" over and over again, and then it started moving in a figure eight. It was very fast and seemed very aggressive. Then Rachel and I noticed the huge lamp on the end table. We screamed and ran out of the room, followed by the other two. We were afraid that "the spirit" would throw the lamp at us. Well, that was it for me and Ouija boards. It wasn't that scary now that I think about it. I'm not anxious to try it again, but I'm sure I could be pressured into it.

Shannon, a 24-year-old of Irish American descent, described this frightening experience in Endicott, New York, in November 1998. Although she shows some skepticism about "the spirit," she seems to believe that something uncanny is taking place. How can the Ouija board possibly know about a nickname that only she and Katie have shared with each other? After finishing her story, Shannon explains that although she has no desire to use a Ouija board again, others could probably make her do it. For young adults as well as for kids, peer pressure exerts a powerful influence.

Doorway to the Dead

When I was sixteen, my friend and I made a doorway in which we could "communicate" with the dead in the room. He had learned this from family in both Peru and Paraguay. We took six pens, each holding three so that we would be unable to move them ourselves without it being visible that we were doing so. We connected them at the tips to make a sort of rectangle or "doorway." From here we were able to ask any spirits present "yes" or "no" questions. If the doorway contracted on itself it meant no, and if it expanded, it meant yes. From this we learned that it was indeed Nino [the ghost of the man who had died in the house] that was "living" in my room, and that he meant us no harm, just that he was looking or waiting for someone or something.

Jonathan Wickers, a 19-year-old resident of Flushing, New York, narrated this personal experience story in April 2005. His story shows how easily rituals related to the supernatural can travel from one country to another. In Peru and Paraguay, Jonathan's friend learned a new way to communicate with the dead. The two friends believed that the ghost of Nino, a previous resident of the house already known to them as a mover of furniture, an opener of doors, and a breaker of glass light covers, had sent a message by moving the doorway to the dead. This ritual, similar to use of the Ouija board, reassured them that Nino was not dangerous.

MATERIAL CULTURE

Early Plant Lore

An ear-piercing whistle could be constructed from a willow branch, and a particularly disagreeable sound could be evoked by every boy, and (I must acknowledge it) by every girl, too, by placing broad leaves of grass—preferably the pretty striped ribbon-grass, or gardener's garters—between the thumbs and blowing thereon.

Other skilful and girl-envied accomplishments of the boys I will simply name: making baskets and brooches by cutting or filing the furrowed butternut or the stone of a peach; also fairy baskets, Japanesque in workmanship, of cherry stones; manufacturing old-women dolls of hickory nuts; squirt-guns and pop-guns of elderberry stems; pipes of horse-chestnuts, corn-cobs, or acorns, in which dried sweet-fern could be smoked; sweet-fern or grape-stem or corn-silk cigars.

Alice Morse Earle included this summary of children's mastery of plant lore in her book *Child Life in Colonial Days* (390). This passage from the "Flower Lore" chapter of Earle's book demonstrates how skillfully children in eighteenth- and nineteenth-century America created playthings from plants. Earle draws a line between girls' and boys' craftsmanship, finding boys to be better at making dolls, guns, pipes, baskets, and cigars. In another part of the "Flower Lore" chapter she mentions girls' ability to make tiny tea sets from rose hips. This sharp distinction between girls' and boys' material culture mirrors gender roles of the time period that Earle describes. Girls were expected to take an interest in domestic pursuits indoors, while boys could wander freely and smoke with each other outside.

While contemporary children do not make as many plant creations as they did in colonial days, counselors at summer camps teach children nature lore, and rural families maintain certain traditions. Simon J. Bronner's *American Children's Folklore* includes descriptions of hickory-bark whistles and spring guns made

Boy learns to blow through a grass-blade whistle in Maine, 2007. Photograph by Martha Harris.

from an elderberry bush or hickory wood, as well as slingshots and bull roarers made of sticks (202–04).

Plant Lore of the Mid-Twentieth Century

Take a long blade of grass. Cut a slit in the middle. Hold it in your hand and blow through it. You can call cows that way. We used to do that in New Orleans.

Make a slit near the bottom of the stem of the first clover. Take the next clover and insert the head through the slit until you have two chained together. Keep going until you have a necklace, bracelet, or headband. They hold together very well.

To sip honeysuckle, hold the flower between your fingers, like this (holds up two fingers). Then suck on the honeysuckle like the hummingbirds do.

Hold a buttercup under someone's chin to see if the person likes butter. It reflects on your chin if you do.

Blowing on dandelion fluff—we used to do that, but I don't remember why. It was just fun to do.

My sister, Sarah Owens, gave me these explanations of her favorite plant lore in Raymond, Maine, in June 2007. Born in the early 1950s, she grew up in Washington, D.C., Japan, and Maryland and spent her young adulthood in New Orleans.

These reminiscences show great pleasure in learning about nature. In contrast to Alice Morse Earle's description, there is no mention of gender distinctions. Blowing on dandelion fluff often has a connection to wishing. Jeanne R. Chesanow's *Honeysuckle Sipping* (1987) offers many other examples of plant lore of this time period.

Plant Lore of the Twenty-First Century

Jason: (to Berit) Find a good piece of grass that's really thin. Cut it in half, like this. Hold it *tight* between your fingers and blow *hard!*

Berit: (blows through her piece of grass) Like this?

Jason: Good!

Jason, 21 years old, taught his girlfriend, Berit, how to make a grass-blade whistle during Gravity Fest in Munnsville, New York, in July 2007. During the festival, which included street luge and gravity bike races, I watched many children and teenagers making loud noises with grass-blade whistles. It is still fairly common for children to learn how to make grass-blade whistles from friends or relatives, especially in rural areas, but there is also a growing trend toward Web-based instruction that preserves and codifies this form of material culture. Teachers, camp counselors, and children old enough to use the Internet have become accustomed to using Web sites as sources of traditional knowledge.

Chinese Fortune-Tellers

We make Chinese Fortune Tellers at school. In all the little compartments you can put in fortunes, like dirty ones, stupid ones, good ones, and a lot about the boys. They are fun because you can usually use them during the day when the teacher isn't looking. We don't *really* believe in the fortunes, except when they say something really good. But sometimes it comes true. I guess it just depends what colors and numbers you pick.

This description of the paper toys that kids usually call *fortune-tellers* or *cootie catchers* came from 13-year-old Maureen, whose family heritage was Irish American, in Mahopac, New York, in April 1987. The eight fortunes inside her fortune-teller were "Boys think you're pretty," "You won't get married," "You're a good best friend," "Tommy likes you," "You smell," "You're nice," "You'll get married at 23," and "You will marry Michael." As in many jump-rope and autograph rhymes of this era, the main topics are courtship and marriage.

Good and Bad Fortunes

1. You will go on a dayt with a famis person.
2. You will barff.
3. You will get $11,000.
4. You will lose all your money.
5. You will find a gold mind [*sic*].
6. You will lose your hair.
7. You will not get canser.
8. You will start to smoke because somewan corses you.

Folklorist Janet Gilmore found these fortunes inside a paper fortune-teller on the playground of the former third- to sixth-grade school building in Mt. Horeb, Wisconsin, between 1998 and 2001. This set of fortunes consists of four pairs, each of which has one good fortune and one disastrous one. While one fortune predicts a date, the other seven foretell events related to money, hair, smoking, and disease rather than romance: a shift away from the love divination of earlier years.

Snow Fort

There are two ways of making a snow fort in the winter time, depending on the snow. If the snow has a crust you stamp out a circle with your feet, then lift it up. If it's too big it will break. You can stand the crusts on end and cement it together with the snow underneath. The other way is to roll up the snow in balls if the snow is wetter, but it isn't as much fun because it's harder and you can't make a roof.

Amelia, age nine, explained how to build a snow fort in Middletown, Connecticut, in the fall of 1977. As the above text shows, children learn specific skills for constructing snow forts or shelters. Amelia distinguishes between the easier, more pleasant method that works for snow with a crust and the harder, less enjoyable technique that suits wet snow. Since her hometown in Connecticut usually gets a fair amount of snow during the winter, snow craftsmanship there has developed well-defined rules. For more information on children's snow craftsmanship, see Bronner (206–11).

Houses Like Boxes

When we were kids, we used to play on the third floor with couch cushions. We used to play house and we built the houses like boxes and we'd climb into it, and in the end we'd jump on it. It was four square cushions, and we made four walls. We pretended to be in a house, holding it up together. There was no roof.

Nineteen-year-old Peggy, an Asian American resident of Boston, Massachusetts, narrated these reminiscences of childhood house-building during a telephone conversation in February 2006. As in Amelia's description of snow fort construction, the rules for building a couch-cushion house seem clear. Four cushions, held together by the players, form the shape of a box. Although this simple structure has no roof, it helps the children imagine that they are inside a house of their own. Sometimes children cover the top of a couch-cushion house with a blanket or sheet, which gives them more privacy than a house with no roof.

Spaceship Fort

One fort that sticks out in my mind is when we took two couches and put them close to each other and covered the top with blankets. We had one of those learning games (kind of like a giant calculator that you could add on), and we acted as if it were a computer. We pretended our fort was a giant spaceship and would sit for hours pretending to fly around and find things.

I was the navigator, so I would operate the computer, and my cousin Mark was the captain who would steer the ship and lead us. My sister and our other cousin just worked on the ship (being the oldest, Mark and I would assign jobs to the younger two). Our parents would leave us there for hours, and we didn't need TV or anything. There were always tons of tears when it was time to leave. Now my cousin Mark is in the Air Force Academy, and when I think about our fort, I like to think we all sparked his interest in flying when we played in that fort.

Colleen, an Irish American college student from Pearl River, New York, recorded her memories of this exciting game in March 2007. Colleen lived in the Bronx when she played in her spaceship fort at the age of six. Play of this kind can generate interest in future careers as well as providing hours of fun.

WORKS CITED

Abrahams, Roger D. *Jump-Rope Rhymes: A Dictionary.* Austin: U of Texas P, 1969.

Abrahams, Roger D., and Lois Rankin. *Counting-Out Rhymes: A Dictionary.* Austin: U of Texas P, 1980.

Ackerley, Janice. "Gender Issues in the Playground Rhymes of New Zealand Children: 1993–2003." *Children's Folklore Review* 26 (2003–04): 7–62.

———. "Playground Rhymes Keep Up with the Times." *Play and Folklore* 42 (September 2002): 4–8.

A Look at Me: Writings. Brigham City, UT: Intermountain Indian School, 1971.

Arleo, Andy. "The Saga of Susie: The Dynamics of an International Handclapping Game." *Play Today in the Primary School Playground.* Ed. Julia C. Bishop and Mavis Curtis. Buckingham, Eng., and Philadelphia: Open UP, 2001. 115–32.

Armor, Kelly. "Folk Songs of Champions." Compact disc. Erie, PA: Erie Art Museum, 2004.

Barrick, Mac E. "The Newspaper Riddle Joke." *Journal of American Folklore* 87.345 (1974): 253–57.

Beckwith, Martha Warren. *Jamaica Folk-Lore.* 1928. New York: Kraus, 1969.

Bronner, Simon J. *American Children's Folklore*. Little Rock: August, 1988.

Butcher, Liz. "Diarrhea." Fife Folklore Archives, 8A, Group 5, 1.5.5, Winter 1998.

Chagall, Irene. "Let's Get Rhythm." *Children's Folklore Review* 28 (2005–2006): 43–63.

Chesanow, Jeanne R. *Honeysuckle Sipping: The Plant Lore of Childhood*. Camden, ME: Down East Books, 1987.

Chinery, David. "Snooping for Snipes: America's Favorite Wild Goose Chase." *Children's Folklore Review* 10.1 (1987): 3–4.

Cooper, Martha. *Street Play*. New York: From Here to Fame, 2006.

Dargan, Amanda, and Steven Zeitlin. *City Play*. New Brunswick, NJ: Rutgers UP, 1990.

Darian-Smith, Kate, and June Factor, eds. *Child's Play: Dorothy Howard and the Folklore of Australian Children*. Melbourne: Museum Victoria, 2005.

Dégh, Linda. "The Roommate's Death and Other Related Dormitory Stories in Formation." *Indiana Folklore* 2.2 (1969): 55–74.

Douglas, Norman. *London Street Games*. 1916. London: Chatto and Windus, 1931.

Dundes, Alan. "Bloody Mary in the Mirror." *Bloody Mary in the Mirror: Essays in Psychoanalytic Folkloristics*. Ed. Alan Dundes. Jackson: UP of Mississippi, 2002. 76–94.

Earle, Alice Morse. *Child Life in Colonial Days*. New York: Macmillan, 1898.

Ellis, Bill. "'Ralph and Rudy': The Audience's Role in Re-creating a Camp Legend." *Western Folklore* 41 (1982): 169–91.

Fine, Gary Alan. "Folklore Diffusion through Interactive Social Networks: Conduits in a Preadolescent Community." *New York Folklore* 5 (1979): 87–126.

Fowke, Edith. *Sally Go Round the Sun: 300 Songs, Rhymes and Games of Canadian Children*. Toronto: McClelland and Stewart, 1969.

Gaunt, Kyra D. *The Games Black Girls Play: Learning the Ropes from Double-Dutch to Hip-Hop*. New York: New York UP, 2006.

Gimple, Erika. "Children's Song Parodies." Northern Virginia Folklife Archive, 1981–30, October 1981.

Gomme, Alice Bertha. *The Traditional Games of England, Scotland, and Ireland*. 2 vols. 1894–98. New York: Dover, 1964.

Green, Joanne, and J.D.A. Widdowson. *Traditional English Language Genres: Continuity and Change*. Vol. 2. Sheffield: National Centre for English Cultural Tradition, 2003.

Grider, Sylvia Ann. "The Supernatural Narratives of Children." Diss., Indiana U, 1976.

Hall, Gary. "Folkgames." *Introduction to Folklore*. Ed. Robert J. Adams. Columbus: Collegiate, 1973. 70–79.

Hansen, Randall. "School Days, School Days: A Study of Folklore in Southern Utah's Public Schools, 1920-1982." Fife Folklore Archives, Folk Collection 8: USU, box 18: 82-108, Summer 1982.

Haring, Lee, and Mark Breslerman. "The Cropsey Maniac." *New York Folklore* 3.1–4 (1977): 15–27.

Hutchins, Courtney. "Humor Through the Eyes of a Child." Fife Folklore Archives, Folk Collection 8: USU, box 73: 01-035, Spring 2001.

Johnson, Nola. "Collection Project." Northeast Folklore Archive, University of Maine, 217:13. 1967.

Knapp, Mary, and Herbert Knapp. *One Potato, Two Potato: The Secret Education of American Children*. New York: Norton, 1976.

Kvideland, Reimund. "Stories about Death as a Part of Children's Socialization." *Folklore on Two Continents.* Ed. Carl Lindahl and Nikolai Burlakoff. Bloomington: Trickster, 1980. 59–64.

Langlois, Janet. "'Mary Whales, I Believe in You': Myth and Ritual Subdued." *Indiana Folklore* 11.1 (1978): 5–33.

Legman, Gershon. *Rationale of the Dirty Joke: An Analysis of Sexual Humor.* New York: Grove P, 1968.

McDowell, John H. "The Speech Play and Verbal Art of Chicano Children: An Ethnographic and Sociolinguistic Study." Diss., U of Texas at Austin, 1975.

Michaels, Barbara, and Bettye Whyte, *Apples on a Stick: The Folklore of Black Children.* New York: Coward-McCann, 1983.

Miller, Sara. "Children's Folklore Autobiography." Unpublished essay, Binghamton University. March 23, 2007.

Newell, William Wells. *Games and Songs of American Children.* 1883. New York: Dover, 1963.

Opie, Iona, and Peter Opie. *Children's Games in Street and Playground.* Oxford: Clarendon, 1969.

———. *The Lore and Language of Schoolchildren.* New York: Oxford UP, 1959.

———. *The Oxford Dictionary of Nursery Rhymes.* 1951. Oxford: Clarendon, 1973.

———. *The Singing Game.* New York: Oxford UP, 1985.

Posen, I. Sheldon. "Pranks and Practical Jokes at Children's Summer Camps." *Southern Folklore Quarterly* 38 (1974): 299–309.

Randolph, Vance, and May K. McCord. "Autograph Albums in the Ozarks." *Journal of American Folklore* 61.240 (1948): 182–93.

Roemer, Danielle. "A Social Interactional Analysis of Anglo Children's Folklore: Catches and Narratives." Diss., U of Texas at Austin, 1977.

Rush, Judith. "Twin Pranks and Practical Jokes." *Children's Folklore Newsletter* 10.3 (1987): 3–8.

Russell, Heather. *Play and Friendships in a Multi-Cultural Playground.* Melbourne: Australian Children's Folklore Publications, 1986.

Sherman, Josepha, and T.K.F. Weisskopf. *Greasy Grimy Gopher Guts: The Subversive Folklore of Childhood.* Little Rock: August, 1995.

"The Singing Playground." *Museum of Childhood.* 2004. http://www.vam.ac.uk/moc/childrens_lives/holidays_entertainment/the_singing_playground/index.htm.

Smedley, Stephanie. "Children's Folklore of Northern Utah and Southern Idaho." Fife Folklore Archives, Folk Collection 8: USU, box 67: 98-020, Spring 1998.

Starr, Mrs. Morton H. "Wisconsin Pastimes." *Journal of American Folklore* 67.264 (1954): 184.

Staunton, Sara. "Riddle Use and Comprehension in Irish School-Aged Children: A Developmental Study." *Children's Folklore Review* 23.2 (Spring 2001): 7–100.

Sutton-Smith, Brian. "The Kissing Games of Adolescents in Ohio." 1959. *The Folkgames of Children.* Ed. Brian Sutton-Smith. Austin: U of Texas P, 1972. 465–90.

Taggert, Jan. "Jump-Rope Rhymes." Fife Folklore Archives, Folk Collection 8: USU, box 16: 82-087, Spring 1982.

Thomas, Jeannie B. "Dumb Blondes, Dan Quayle and Hillary Clinton: Gender, Sexuality and Stupidity in Jokes." *Journal of American Folklore* 110.437 (1997): 277–313.

Tucker, Elizabeth. *Campus Legends: A Handbook.* Westport, CT: Greenwood, 2005.

———. "Cropsey at Camp." *Voices: The Journal of New York Folklore* 32.3–4 (2006): 42.

———. "Tradition and Creativity in the Storytelling of Pre-Adolescent Girls." Diss., Indiana U, 1977.

———. "'I Hate You, You Hate Me': Children's Responses to Barney the Dinosaur." *Children's Folklore Review* 22.1 (1999): 25–33.

Virtanen, Leea. *Children's Lore.* Studia Fennica 22. Helsinki: Suomalisen Kirjallisuuden Seura, 1978.

Vlach, John. "One Black Eye and Other Horrors: A Case for the Humorous Anti-Legend." *Indiana Folklore* 4 (1971): 95–140.

Weiss, Halina. "*Draznilkas*—Russian Children's Taunts." *Slavic and East European Folklore Association Journal* 4.2 (Spring 1999): 35–46.

Williams, Melissa. "Children's Playground Games." Fife Folklore Archives, Folk Collection 8: USU, box 67: 98-024, April 1998.

Four
Scholarship and Approaches

FOUNDING SCHOLARS

William Wells Newell's *Games and Songs of American Children* (1883) first identified children's folklore as a separate area of study. Before the publication of Newell's book, a few other scholars had published books on children's lore. Joseph Strutt's *Sports and Pastimes of the People of England* (1801) includes some boys' games of skill and a few girls' games; Robert Chambers's *Popular Rhymes of Scotland* (1826) and James Halliwell's *Nursery Rhymes of England* (1842) and *Popular Rhymes and Nursery Tales of England* (1849) examine rhymes and tales taught to young children. Newell's study takes a different approach. Observing children's play and commenting insightfully on its meaning, Newell considers children on their own terms. His book still delights readers of the twenty-first century.

After his graduation from Harvard Divinity School in 1863, Newell worked as a minister and as an employee of the War Department in Washington, D.C.; in the early 1870s he founded a school in New York. Early in the 1880s, he retired from employment to pursue his diverse interests as an independent scholar. At that point he had enough free time to observe and record children's street games in New York City. In 1888, he cofounded the American Folklore Society and became the first editor of the *Journal of American Folklore*.

Newell's *Games and Songs of American Children* does not simply describe children's folklore; it also identifies its purposes and places it in the context of previous scholarship. In his introduction to the Dover edition of the book, published in 1963, Carl Withers explains that Newell's organization of children's games into categories was "a remarkable and imaginative pioneer thrust toward what was later to be called 'functionalism'" (vi). This insight, contributed by folklorist

Herbert Halpert, helps us understand how Newell's innovative study inspired later functionalist studies in the field of children's folklore.

Shortly after the publication of Newell's *Games and Songs,* the British folklorist Lady Alice Bertha Gomme produced an impressive study of children's games. Gomme, wife of anthropologist Sir George Laurence Gomme, was a founding member of the Folk-Lore Society and Folk-Song Society in England. She published her two-volume *Traditional Games of England, Scotland, and Ireland* between 1894 and 1898. This study of about 800 games from 112 locations in the United Kingdom gives the reader a prodigious amount of information about children's traditions from the middle to the end of the nineteenth century. Her commentary on game variants follows the evolutionary approach that was common in the 1890s. Closely examining game-playing patterns, Gomme looked for survivals of early rituals. She concluded that the singing game "London Bridge Is Falling Down" represented ancient sacrifices in the foundations of bridges, while courting games such as Nuts in May represented an early form of "marriage by capture" (2: 484).

Some twentieth-century scholars have downplayed Gomme's achievements, finding her evolutionary approach limiting and disappointing. In his study *The British Folklorists,* Richard M. Dorson wryly states that Gomme followed her

Girls play a singing game in New York City in the late 1970s. Photograph by Martha Cooper.

husband's academic preferences with "perfect conjugal accord" (280). Iona and Peter Opie recognize the value of her large collection of game texts but criticize her search for survivals (*Singing Game* v–vi). According to Dorothy Howard, Gomme "chose to ignore the games of Dickens' illiterate back alleys and tenements though she could have hardly been unaware that they existed." This critical comment seems minor, however, in view of Howard's assertion that "No student of children's playlore can now or ever ignore the Gomme *Dictionary*. No monumental study equal to hers has yet appeared anywhere" ("Introduction" vi, viii).

Within the past 20 years, folklorists have found other strengths in Gomme's work. In her essay "Alice Bertha Gomme (1852–1938): A Reassessment of the Work of a Folklorist" (1990), Georgina Boyes praises Gomme's "reasoned and sophisticated" analysis and her adherence to "rigorous academic standards" that surpassed the standards of William Wells Newell (199–200). One of Gomme's greatest achievements, Boyes argues, is her close attention to girls' games and to games played by adolescents. Cocklebread, for example, is a game in which adolescent girls "wabble to and fro with their Buttocks" (Gomme 1: 74–76). Gomme deserves credit for describing the details of this game, which some adults of that era would not have found appropriate for open discussion.

PLAYGROUND PIONEERS

Iona and Peter Opie, who began their long and fruitful career as a husband-and-wife research team with the publication of *I Saw Esau: Traditional Rhymes of Youth* (1947), demonstrated the importance of studying children's traditions through a dazzling array of publications. Their *Oxford Dictionary of Nursery Rhymes* (1952) quickly became the canonical work on the subject of nursery lore. Seven years later, in 1959, their *Lore and Language of Schoolchildren* presented jokes, riddles, jeers, customs, beliefs, narratives, and other kinds of folklore from 5,000 children in England, Scotland, Ireland, and Wales. Immensely readable, erudite, and entertaining, this important book showed a large international audience the richness and variety of children's traditions.

Although *The Lore and Language of Schoolchildren* is the Opies' best-known work, their *Children's Games in Street and Playground* (1969) provides an invaluable classification and analysis of games. Among the game categories scrutinized in this detailed study are chasing, catching, hunting, seeking, racing, exerting, dueling, guessing, daring, acting, and pretending. Folklorists have benefited greatly from the wide range of descriptive, comparative, and analytical content of this important study. Similarly, *The Singing Game* (1985) presents texts and tunes of games of this genre in remarkable depth and detail.

Peter Opie passed away in 1982, but Iona Opie has continued to publish significant works. Her book *The People in the Playground* (1993) chronicles weekly visits to a London playground, beginning in 1970. Her openness in portraying the children exactly as they are—as full-fledged people, not just schoolchildren—makes this book a delight to read. She has also published other books for children and adults.

Brian Sutton-Smith, one of the most influential and dedicated scholars in the field of children's folklore, began his career as a primary school teacher in Wellington, New Zealand, in 1948. From 1949 to 1951, he gathered information about children's play and games for his doctoral dissertation while visiting 35 New Zealand schools. In his "Play Biography" (1997–98), Sutton-Smith explains that he did his research while "traveling free all over the country, up and down the mountains, due to the courtesy of school physical education specialists, and often sleeping overnight in their cars which were sometimes frosted over in the morning" (5). Compiling information from more than a thousand child and adult informants, he assembled a record of New Zealand play and games that eventually took the form of two books: *The Games of New Zealand Children* (1959) and *A History of Children's Play: The New Zealand Playground* (1981).

During long periods of observation on New Zealand playgrounds, Sutton-Smith learned that each playground was "a place which mostly ran itself" ("Play Biography" 15). Social play and power relationships formed the crux of playground life, which needed very little intervention from adults. In somewhat different terms, Sutton-Smith observed that the playground was "something like a frontier society controlled from a distance by a lurking Sheriff/Teacher or two" ("Play Biography" 16). With minimal adult intervention, children could keep order, handle bullies, and take care of all but the most serious problems on their own.

Sutton-Smith's many publications have contributed enormously to folklorists' understanding of children's play, games, and narratives. Among his most influential works are *The Folkgames of Children* (1972) and *The Folkstories of Children* (1981). His relatively recent book *The Ambiguity of Play* (1998) examines play theory from the standpoint of seven rhetorics: fate, power, communal identity, frivolity, progress, the imaginary, and the self. This exciting, innovative study suggests possible directions for a new science of play for our current era.

One of the most important pioneers of children's folklore study, Dorothy Howard, broke new ground in her doctoral research at New York University. When she chose children's folklore as the subject of her 1938 dissertation "Folk Jingles of American Children," she had to overcome opposition from the professors on her committee. Her focus on rhymes collected directly from children influenced the work of other folklorists, including Iona and Peter Opie, according to Jonathan Cott. Howard came to Australia in 1954 to study children's games as a postdoctoral Fulbright scholar. Her articles on Australian children's variants of Hopscotch, Knucklebones, ball-bouncing, marbles, and rhymes of various kinds give the reader an excellent sense of the games' and rhymes' complexity. When

Howard was traveling across Australia to collect her material, families were struggling to overcome the effects of World War II, and television had not yet arrived. Brian Sutton-Smith's essay "Courage in the Playground: A Tribute to Dorothy Howard" emphasizes the originality and courage of Howard's work. *Child's Play: Dorothy Howard and the Folklore of Australian Children* (2005), edited by Kate Darian-Smith and June Factor, explicates Howard's contributions to children's folklore in detail, with interesting photographs and diagrams.

Another innovative scholar, Nigel Kelsey, became interested in children's folklore while training to become a teacher during World War II. During his 30-year teaching career (1952–82), he worked as a primary-school teacher, deputy head teacher, and head teacher at several schools in London. In 1964 he began writing down and tape-recording rhymes and game descriptions. While doing research on children's speech and creative writing for the Diploma in the Education of Children at the University of London, Kelsey put children at ease by asking them for rhymes, jokes, riddles, tongue twisters, and games. His retirement in 1982 gave him the chance to begin an ambitious collection of children's folklore at 20 schools in the London area. According to Robin Wiltshire, this collection yielded more than 30 tape recordings that included numerous skipping, clapping, and ball-bouncing rhymes, as well as singing games, action and dance routines, song parodies, taunts, limericks, puzzles, riddles, and jokes.

Kelsey published a number of articles in prestigious folklore journals; his essay "Norman Douglas Revisited" (1983) points out relationships between games in his own inner-city London collection and games collected in London by Douglas in 1916. Kelsey did not publish his book manuscript, titled *"Everybody Gather Round": A Study of Inner London Children's Folklore 1982–1984 (Plus Some Lore Collected from a Few Inner London Schools 1960–1981)*. Professor J.D.A. Widdowson, director of the Centre for English Cultural Tradition and Language at the University of Sheffield, worked with Kelsey until his death in 1990 and agreed to edit the book. This important publication, titled *Everybody Gather Round*, will include games, school rhymes and parodies, teases and taunts, superstitions, nonsense rhymes, jokes, riddles, tongue twisters, limericks, puzzles, songs, chants, and other material from the treasure trove of inner-city London children's folklore.

PERFORMANCE

In the late 1960s, emphasis on the context surrounding folklore texts gave birth to the performance school of folklore study. Dan Ben-Amos's article "Toward a Definition of Folklore in Context" explains that scholars should pay attention to such contextual elements as place, time, and company (11). Roger Abrahams, another eloquent advocate of performance study, makes the point that "performance, item, and audience" are all equally significant (143–58).

Performance studies tend to follow a cross-disciplinary approach, emphasizing the need for detailed ethnographies and linguistic analysis.

Kenneth S. Goldstein's "Strategy in Counting-Out: An Ethnographic Folklore Field Study" clearly demonstrates the importance of doing ethnographies of children's games that provide data for analyzing performance. Getting to know 67 children in Philadelphia from 1966 to 1967, Goldstein discovered that their counting-out rhymes to choose sides or determine who would be "it" involved complex strategy. When he asked the children why they used counting-out rhymes, most of them explained that the rhymes gave them all equal chances. As they performed counting-outs, however, the children used certain strategies to influence who got chosen: choosing a particular rhyme, adding extra words, skipping regular counts, stopping or continuing, and changing positions. These results proved that "for some children 'counting-out' is a game of strategy rather than chance" and indicated that using similar methods to reexamine other games would be a good idea (178).

Richard Bauman's "Ethnography of Children's Folklore" argues against "adultocentrism" and for exploration of "the place and uses of folklore in the conduct of social life and the competence that underlies this use" (174). Bauman praises "the truly impressive range of linguistic and sociolinguistic competencies that is fostered by the children's own peer group culture" (184). In his discussion of catch routines, he notes that children's "striking awareness of sociolinguistic nuances" playfully promotes social disorder (181). Instead of identifying "knock knock" interactions as jokes, he suggests that they should be called "solicitational routines": a term that emphasizes social interaction rather than simple humor (177).

Bauman's direction of dissertations by Children's Folklore Project participants at the University of Texas at Austin resulted in significant studies of children's performance of riddles, jokes, catch routines, and narratives. John H. McDowell's "Speech Play and Verbal Art of Chicano Children: An Ethnographic and Sociolinguistic Study" (1975) presents children's interaction in detail, distinguishing among descriptive routines, riddles, and routines of victimization, among other categories; his attention to poetic form also offers valuable information. In a somewhat similar vein, Danielle Roemer's "Social Interactional Analysis of Anglo Children's Folklore: Catches and Narratives" (1977) closely examines the verbal artistry of children aged five to nine in the Austin community. Roemer's insightful analysis of catch routines gives the children involved in each routine the roles of "trickster" and "straightman." She explains that "dirty" and "nasty" catch routines and narratives let children explore forbidden subjects while maintaining "implicit conventions and expectations" (35).

Gary Alan Fine's "Rude Words: Insults and Narration in Preadolescent Obscene Talk" examines children's use of obscenity in the context of conversation. During his fieldwork with children in New England and Minnesota over a three-year period, Fine learned that it was often possible to distinguish between rude talk as interaction (insults) and as narration (53). Face-to-face insults differ from insults toward someone who is not present; some insults take the form of playful repartee, with no malicious intent. Some obscene narrations emphasize the speaker's linguistic skill; others focus more on joking or on sexual instruction. Fine makes the important point that "the jokes which are told in natural contexts are not carefully polished productions, such as we read in jokebooks" (61). By reading full texts of conversations, we can gain a better understanding of interactions of this kind.

PSYCHOANALYTIC APPROACHES

Scholars who have applied Sigmund Freud's psychoanalytic theory to children's folklore have focused primarily on jokes, rituals, and legends. Martha Wolfenstein's study *Children's Humor* (1954) explains that children use jokes to transform painful situations into laughter. A sequence of dirty jokes shows how children of different ages handle sexual and scatological humor: A four-year-old likes to shout "Hello, Mr. Doody!"; children between the ages of 7 and 11 enjoy jokes that involve simple wordplay; and children 11 or older have the ability to use language in more sophisticated ways (161–65). Wolfenstein explains that the joke façade, which masks sexual and hostile content, works better as children get older. Mastery of the joke façade brings "not only pleasure in virtuosity, but momentary triumph over inhibition, and the response of others" (191).

Another study of humor related to children is Gershon Legman's remarkably thorough *Rationale of the Dirty Joke* (1968), the first chapter of which is devoted to children. Scrutinizing hostile impulses reflected in jokes, Legman suggests that "Under the mask of humor, our society allows infinite aggressions, by everyone and against everyone" (1). He finds that jokes about children reflect penis envy, ridicule, sexual starvation, and a desire to put others on the spot, as well as eagerness to learn about sexual matters. Unfortunately, Legman does not specify the age of his informants; it appears that most of the jokes in his chapter about children come from adults. A better source of information about children's dirty joke patterns is Rosemary Zumwalt's essay "Plain and Fancy: A Content Analysis of Children's Jokes Dealing with Adult Sexuality."

The leader of American psychoanalytic studies of children's folklore was Alan Dundes, whose publications extend from the 1960s to the early twenty-first century. In his essay "On the Psychology of Legend" (1971), Dundes analyzes teenage girls' renditions of the popular legend "The Hook." The crux of this legend is a teenage couple hearing, while parked in Lovers' Lane, a radio announcement that a sex maniac with a hook in the place of a hand has escaped from an insane asylum. Teenage boys, Dundes suggests, may be "all hands" while parking with girlfriends. The hook, a phallic symbol, represents girls' fears of losing control. After the girl begs to go home, the boy "pulls out" and drives her home. Reaching out to open the door on her side of the car, he finds a hook hanging from the door's handle. The hook's removal from the sex maniac's body symbolizes castration of the boy, who has lost his chance for sexual experimentation (30–31).

One of Dundes's most interesting studies of children's lore is "The Dead Baby Joke Cycle," published in 1979. Examining a sample of teenagers' jokes from the 1960s and 1970s, Dundes asserts that "there is a sick streak—and a longstanding one at that—in American humor" (145). He notes that "Little Willie" rhymes from 1899 to the 1930s and subsequent "Little Audrey" jokes humorously describe children's deaths. Most dead-baby jokes take the form of questions with answers. Dundes identifies the most common dead-baby joke as "What's red and sits in a corner? A baby chewing (teething on, eating, sucking on) razor blades" (151). Among the reasons for these jokes' popularity, Dundes cites teenagers' tension about sexual activity and concern about unwanted pregnancies. It is possible, he suggests, that gross dead-baby jokes give teenagers "one way of fighting the fear and gilding the guilt" (154). Addressing some adults' distaste for these jokes, Dundes wisely states, "If anything is sick, it is the society which produces sick humor. Eliminating the humor—even if such censorship were possible, which it definitely is not—would not solve the problems which led to the generation of the folklore in the first place" (155). Another psychoanalytic essay by Dundes, "Bloody Mary in the Mirror," is discussed in the "Supernatural" section of this chapter.

In "The Magic of the Boy Scout Campfire" (1980), Jay Mechling applies psychoanalytic theory to campfire rituals of Boy Scouts in California. Mechling identifies six elements of the campfire event: its opening (marked by the lighting of the fire), songs, skits, yells, tales, and closing. Defining the campfire site as "almost sacred space," he finds that the fire has sexual significance (50). Freud's 1932 essay "The Acquisition and Control of Fire" suggests that to gain control over fire, men had to stop themselves from urinating on it. Mechling finds that Boy Scouts' "fire fun," including building, lighting, and urinating on a fire, supports a psychoanalytic interpretation of campfire rituals' significance. He concludes that the Boy Scout campfire event is "a ritual dramatization of male solidarity and male world view" (56). The fact that Girl Scouts also enjoy campfires does not undermine this interpretation, since "fire is a multivocal symbol that functions differently in the two contexts, male and female" (55).

GENDER

Scholarship on gender issues in children's folklore has grown significantly since the 1970s. In his article "The Play of Girls" (1979), Brian Sutton-Smith notes that boys and girls tend to play different kinds of games within different kinds of play groups, but that there are "many more forms of play that the sexes share than used to be the case" (250). Anthropologists, sociologists, and psychologists, as well as folklorists, have analyzed how boys and girls learn about gender through play, sometimes discovering sharp contrasts between boys and girls. In some studies, researchers have found relatively few differences. Rivka Eifermann's study of thousands of children in Israel in 1971, for example, notes that most games of that time and place cannot be called "boys' games" or "girls' games."

Studies comparing groups of boys with groups of girls have given us insight into gender-related play, games, and rituals. Linda Riley's "Extremes: How Girls Play Slaughter, How Boys Play Slaughter at Valley Oak Elementary" (1990), for example, examines differences between boys' and girls' versions of a ball game similar to Dodge Ball. In the game of Slaughter, two teams line up facing each other; the goalie of one team throws a lightweight ball at members of the opposing team. If any member of that team fails to dodge the ball or to throw it back, he or she is "slaughtered" and changes places with the goalie. Riley finds that all-girl teams playing Slaughter in Davis, California, "stress order, egalitarian relationships, and female behavior," while all-boy teams "stress disorder, hierarchical relationships, and male behavior" (16). Both of these gender- related forms of the game reflect social roles and attitudes. Riley suggests that children's game playing has its own momentum, regardless of adult intervention: "The children at Valley Oak Elementary will continue to play Slaughter in their own way because children's games belong to children" (16).

Marjorie Harness Goodwin's study "The Serious Side of Jump Rope" (1985) argues that girls' interaction while jumping rope has continuity with their interactions outside the frame of play. Girls' patterning of conflict shows "specifically female rather than male ways of speaking," with brief arguments about rules (316). Girls argue about who will turn the jump rope, what rhymes will be recited, and what moves should go with each rhyme, balancing criticism of each other with positive remarks. Goodwin concludes that although people have questioned girls' ability to argue without stopping their play, "girls are quite able to handle conflict without disruption of the ongoing interaction" (326).

In another detailed study of girls' game playing, "'You Have to Do It with Style': Girls' Games and Girls' Gaming" (1993), Linda Hughes suggests that *what children play is less important than how they play*. Examining gender distinctions in previous studies of children's games, she finds that scholars tend to characterize boys' games as active, competitive, aggressive, and physical, while they tend to characterize girls' games as cooperative, passive, verbal, and symbolic. Hughes makes the interesting point that Jean Piaget's *Moral Judgment of the Child* connects cooperation to the development of cognitive growth, but some recent studies associate cooperative, relationship-centered play with ineffective development in relation to conflict and competition (133).

While watching 40 children playing the ball-bouncing game Foursquare at a Quaker school near Philadelphia over a period of two years, Hughes got to know

10 girls who were regular players. She found that traditional ideas of girls' "niceness" do not inhibit competitive play; instead, they offer an acceptable framework for competition. Hughes's informants explain that it is possible to "be nice" (by helping other players get back into the game, for example) but not to be extremely nice to everyone; if they are "*really* nice" and never get other players "out," they will be "mean" to others hoping to enter the game, and the game will become boring. By being "nice-mean" and maintaining friendship with each other, the girls make the game successful, competitive, and rewarding (139–40). This nuanced study demonstrates the importance of closely examining how girls and boys play games "to provide a counterpoint to the rhetoric of contrast, difference, and deficit" (144).

Other important insights come from Elizabeth Grugeon's delightful essay "'We Like Singing the Spice Girl Songs…and We Like Tig and Stuck in the Mud': Girls' Traditional Games on Two Playgrounds." During visits to two primary-school playgrounds in the United Kingdom in 1997, Grugeon discovered that the Spice Girls, a popular singing group, had become part of girls' game playing. At the first school that she visited, the Spice Girls' influence had been so strong that school administrators had banned all play related to the singers Ginger Spice, Posh Spice, Sporty Spice, Scary Spice, and Baby Spice. Administrators at the second school, however, welcomed Spice Girl play and told Grugeon that the girls had "asked for a Spice Girl corner" (107). Although the girls at the second school loved to sing "Wannabe" and other Spice Girl songs, Grugeon concluded that performances of the songs were no more significant than any other game played on the playground (113). What mattered most was for the girls to have "break time" (recess) when they could enjoy both traditional games and performances of material adapted from the mass media.

Ethnographic studies of adolescents have demonstrated the complexity of peer-group negotiation during the teen years. In "'Poxy Cupid!' An Ethnographic and Feminist Account of a Resistant Female Youth Culture: The New Wave Girls," Shane J. Blackman explores the dynamics of 10 secondary-school girls in the south of England in the 1980s. Wearing "confrontational" clothes and favoring new wave, punk, reggae, and dub music, the New Wave Girls reject traditional standards of feminine beauty. They resist control by teachers, parents, and boys, "skiving" (skipping school) and trying to gain independence at home. Among their in-group rituals are taping evening conversations, sleeping together in one room, and making burping and farting noises while reminiscing about going to camp. While they are at school, the girls use various methods for repelling obnoxious boys, including putting tampons in their mouths and saying that they are menstruating. Other students at their school spread rumors and tell stories about the New Wave Girls' nefarious activities. Blackman's ethnographic study offers insight into the traditions and rituals of a group of teenage girls, showing how resistance to norms at school and at home brings the girls a sense of power and satisfaction.

Girl plays Hopscotch in Maine in the summer of 2007.
Photograph by Martha Harris.

In "Boys Who Play Hopscotch: The Historical Divide of a Gender Space" (1998), Derek Van Rheenan traces the historical transformation of Hopscotch from a game primarily played by boys to a feminine game "where manly boys dare not tread." Very young boys ("tykes"), older boys who want to disrupt girls' play ("teasers"), and occasional older boys who do not care about the social stigma of entering a feminine space make others more aware of the gender order that exists on the playground Although this gendered terrain has certain traditions, it is possible to play with and resist accepted social structures. Van Rheenan suggests that children function as "active social agents" and that adults need to leave children free to create or re-create culture in their own play areas, without imposition of adult biases (21–23).

SPACE AND PLACE

Children's concepts of space and place have drawn scholars' interest since the second half of the twentieth century. In *Children's Games in Street and Playground*, Iona and Peter Opie identify the most common spaces for children's play, including "the asphalt expanses of school playgrounds, the cage-like enclosures filled with junk by a local authority, the corners of recreation grounds stocked with swings and slides" (12). With unerring wisdom, the Opies recognize children's preference for playing in streets, woods, empty lots, and other areas that are free from adult supervision. They quote a letter written by an 11-year-old British boy in 1955: "In my neighbourhood the sites of Hitler's bombs are many, and the bigger sites with a certain amount of rubble provide very good grounds for Hide and Seek and Tin Can Tommy" (15). Places devastated by war can be especially significant play spaces, as they give children the chance to take creative control of an area marred by destruction and loss of life.

Bernard Mergen's essay "Children's Lore in Schools and Playgrounds" offers an excellent overview of children's play spaces since the mid-nineteenth century, as well as insights into transformation of physical space through play. Mergen makes the important point that "for children, play space is a continuum" (230). Between home and school, many areas serve as play spaces. Mergen cites Roger Hart's innovational study *Children's Experience of Place,* which explores parents' decisions to give their offspring certain levels of freedom and children's preferences to visit certain kinds of spaces. His summary of changes in playground design, location, and size provides a helpful resource for researchers (238–49).

Marc Armitage's "The Ins and Outs of School Playground Play: Children's Use of 'Play Places'" analyzes children's use of playground space at primary schools in the United Kingdom. The primary-school playground, Armitage observes, is "full of imagination, fantasy and mystery; friendship groups; organized and highly structured games; quiet, reflective play; and noise and movement" (37). The typical primary-school playground, an undifferentiated rectangle or square, leaves children free to choose areas for different kinds of play unless teachers intervene. At some schools, players of football (known as soccer in the United States) have taken so much playground space that teachers have had to limit the space available for it. L- or U-shaped playgrounds accommodate different games more easily, so they generate less conflict.

An especially interesting aspect of Armitage's study is his observation of children's creativity in choosing spaces for certain games and imaginative play. On many playgrounds, metal drain covers become boards for games of marbles; some drain covers become known as very challenging surfaces for such games. Metal fences and vertical metal bars become playground "jails," where prisoners in the game Cops and Robbers get locked up. Some of the youngest children play imaginative games involving witches and monsters, which may necessitate making "cauldrons" (holes in the ground or in bench tops, logs, or tables) near the area known as the witch's home. Sometimes a metal door becomes known as the witch's "furnace," where bad children get incinerated (46–54).

Folklorists also learn about children's awareness of space by analyzing narratives. In my essay "Concepts of Space in Children's Narratives," I examine folktales

told by preadolescent girls in the 1970s. Stories from girls of that age group reveal "a predilection for space that is vertical or horizontal, heavily shadowed or
brightly lighted, extremely dangerous or comfortably benign" (19). Because safe
areas are clearly differentiated from dangerous ones in these stories, the young
narrators can feel secure as they tell and listen to scary stories. The typical setting for preadolescent girls' tales is a family's house with at least two floors, as
well as a basement and an attic. Like a castle, which Max Lüthi identifies as the
folktale's central image, this multilevel family home becomes a dominant spatial
framework in preadolescents' tales (Lüthi 166). Within that house, the central
character hears ghostlike noises and goes upstairs or downstairs to confront the
ghostly presence. Sometimes the ghost comes upstairs to pursue the hapless child:
not rapidly, but with slow, measured steps. Adolescents tell stories about dangers
encountered in lover's lanes and a variety of other settings, but for preadolescents,
space within the house matters most. This house is "the child's castle, the shelter-
ing but threatening structure where fear must be mastered before she ventures
forth into the outside world" (24).

Sylvia Grider's essay "The Haunted House in Literature, Popular Culture, and
Tradition" (1999) clarifies the significance of haunted houses for children and
adults. Grider explains how Lüthi's enchanted castle differs from the haunted house:
"The enchanted castle is bright and shining; the haunted house is dark and brood-
ing. The enchanted castle is filled with music and laughter; the haunted house
contains evil and frightening, mysterious noises. The lines of the enchanted castle
are geometrically precise and the perspective is reliable; the haunted house is
skewed and out of focus" (175). While the enchanted castle has been a promi-
nent folktale feature for many centuries, the haunted house can be traced back
to dark, mysterious castles of gothic novels; in the United States, abandoned or
seldom-used mansions built in the Gilded Age inspire narratives about haunting.
Since some of these mansions have become funeral homes, their connection to
ghost stories makes perfect sense (176–80). In ghost stories told by children, the
attics and basements of haunted houses provide settings for ghosts' appearances.
Since the basement is "below the ground, in contact with the forces of the under-
world," it has more potential to frighten children than the attic does (190).

THE SUPERNATURAL

Ever since the Opies identified the "curiosity" of levitation and "half-belief" in
charms and rituals, children's folklore scholars have tried to explain why the supernatural exerts such fascination (*Lore and Language* 206, 309–10). Like games
of danger and sexual experimentation, supernatural rituals push back known
boundaries to investigate the unknown. Unlike other kinds of folklore, however,

rituals related to the supernatural offer a unique kind of excitement: communication with spirits of the dead. While attempts to reach spirits thrill young participants, they also terrify some of them.

Bill Ellis's *Raising the Devil* (2000) and *Lucifer Ascending* (2004) provide important information about the folk cultural context for children's supernatural rituals, including mirror gazing, table setting, Ouija board use, and rumors about Satanic cults' nefarious activities. His chapter "The Devil Worshipers at the Prom" in *Aliens, Ghosts, and Cults* (2003) offers important insight into adolescents' expressive behavior in relation to traumatic suicide and rumors of Satanic cult activity (199–219). Another chapter of the same book, "What Really Happened at Gore Orphanage," identifies adolescents' trips to haunted places as rituals of rebellion that "say 'screw you' to law and order" (188). In *Lucifer Ascending,* Ellis insightfully compares contemporary teenagers' legend-trip behavior to youths' merrymaking at neolithic monuments and cemeteries in the Middle Ages (112–41). Legend trips involve *ostension,* the acting out of legends' content.

Without leaving their homes, children can enjoy the excitement of levitation and trance sessions, described by Mary and Herbert Knapp in *One Potato, Two Potato* (252). My essay "Levitation and Trance Sessions at Preadolescent Girls' Slumber Parties" (1984) examines girls' levitation and trance sessions in southern Indiana and New York between 1976 and 1984. This essay suggests that "preadolescent girls are experimenting with their own power to regulate the intriguing, sometimes threatening awareness of their own development" (133).

In *Children's Lore* (1978), Leea Virtanen describes Finnish children's use of a Ouija board and glass to get answers to questions that seem to come from Satan. Part of the preparation for Finnish children's Ouija board sessions is removal of all catechisms, hymnbooks, and Bibles from the room. Children begin with simple questions, then ask more frightening questions such as when they will die. Virtanen suggests that what happens during Ouija board sessions is "a form of psychic automatism, an activity not dependent on normal consciousness. One of those present directs the course of the glass by his unconscious muscular movements and the other participants interpret these messages from his subconscious as emanating from an outside agency—spirits or the devil" (80–81). Virtanen notes that Finnish adults no longer tell stories about Satan or practice magic to keep him under control, but children maintain a lively interest in this subject.

One of the most widespread rituals practiced by children since the 1970s has been the summoning of a frightening female spirit in a bathroom mirror. Janet Langlois identifies this pattern in her 1978 essay "'Mary Whales, I Believe in You': Myth and Ritual Subdued." Legends about a girl who dies in a car accident after getting terrible facial abrasions emphasize passivity; after her death, the girl appears on a certain street corner in Indianapolis, asks some boys for a ride, then disappears from their car. The accident victim's name is Mary Whales, Mary

Worth, or Mary Lou, among other possibilities. When a child summons the ghost of this unfortunate girl, the ghost becomes an aggressive attacker, inflicting scratches on the face of the young person who dares to summon her. Some children say that Mary Worth or Whales is a witch who died in Salem; others say that she died at the hands of a jealous lover or that she can foretell the future (9, 30).

Since Langlois's identification of this fascinating set of interrelated legends and rituals, other scholars have studied their meaning. Bengt af Klintberg's intriguing essay "'Black Madame, Come Out!'" (1988) quotes a 10-year-old Swedish girl's description of Black Madame (Svarta Madame), who appears in a bathroom mirror after someone says "I don't believe in you, Black Madame" 12 times: "she has green hair and red teeth and luminous yellow eyes; she herself is black" (155). Black Madame is not the only name for spirits of this kind in Sweden; alternate names are Bloody Black Madame, White Madame, Dirty Madame, and Creepy Madame. Swedish children began summoning spirits known by such English names as Mary and Black Molly in bathroom mirrors in the 1970s, but the term Svarta Madame became dominant. Results of Black Madame's appearance vary, but she is commonly associated with good luck, bad luck, and, in the worst-case scenario, sudden death. Af Klintberg concludes that this ritual originated in European fortune-telling games such as mirror gazing in previous centuries. Like television screens, mirrors provide "windows into the unknown" (162–64). In Sweden, children tend to downplay Black Madame's seriousness: "Swedish child culture (and adult culture) is probably generally more dismissive of spirits than the American" (166).

Psychoanalytic analysis gives the summoning of ghosts in mirrors another dimension of meaning. In his essay "Bloody Mary in the Mirror," Alan Dundes suggests that "Bloody Mary" rituals reflect girls' anxiety as they approach puberty. According to Dundes, "the Bloody Mary ritual is a prepubescent fantasy about the imminent onset of menses." Central to his argument is the Freudian premise that blood flowing from the head represents "upwards displacement" of blood from the urinogenital area (87). Dundes presents 10 texts from female narrators and considers other texts from the Knapps' collection of "Scaries" in One Potato, Two Potato (242), as well as Simon J. Bronner's sample of "Mary Worth Rituals" in American Children's Folklore (168–69).

Although Dundes finds the "Bloody Mary" ritual to be closely connected to preadolescent girls, other scholars' analyses have found the ritual to be significant for both boys and girls. In Legend and Belief (2001), Linda Dégh presents a long, detailed "Mary Worth" text collected by Sue Samuelson from an 18-year-old boy (243–44). This text and others support Dégh's contention that "the key in this legend is believing and trusting" (244). My own essay "Ghosts in Mirrors" (2005) views this legend/ritual complex through a somewhat different lens, suggesting that the ritual primarily offers an opportunity for "daring and testing"

Teenagers play with Ouija board in Maine in the fall of 2007. Photograph by Martha Harris.

(187) by both preadolescents and college students. While preadolescence and the college years differ in many ways, both include fear tests that facilitate greater independence and a more complex sense of self.

Few folklorists have studied children's folklore of the supernatural outside of Western culture. Margaret Brady's *"Some Kind of Power": Navajo Children's Skinwalker Narratives* (1984) offers important insight into Navajo children's perceptions of the supernatural. Skinwalkers—witches that wear animal skins—often appear as characters in Navajo children's legends and personal experience stories. At slumber parties and campouts on the reservation, children tell skinwalker stories along with such traditional Anglo-American ghost stories as "The Golden Arm" (100–101). Telling skinwalker stories maintains social boundaries, both by affirming that the teller is not a witch and by suggesting the need for a ceremony to counteract the effects of witchcraft (50).

CROSS-CULTURAL COMPARISON

An excellent cross-cultural study that serves as a model for other research is Andy Arleo's essay "The Saga of Susie: The Dynamics of an International Handclapping Game." Analyzing the international diffusion of the clapping game "When Susie Was a Baby," Arleo considers variants from 10 countries in six languages: English,

French, Danish, Greek, Afrikaans, and Spanish. Most of these variants trace the life of Susie, a lively and spirited young woman, from birth through death and the afterlife. Only the Spanish variants begin with courtship, and only the Australian variants give Susie a profession. For many young chanters of the "Susie" rhyme, the courtship line "Ooh, ah, lost my bra" is the most exciting part (119). The text of one variant including this line is can be found in chapter 3. Arleo summarizes other scholars' conclusions regarding the "Susie" game, including Marilyn Jorgensen's observation that handclapping and jump-rope rhymes give girls a chance to envision their future roles as girlfriends, wives, and mothers (Jorgensen 63).

Carefully considering linguistic and cultural factors, as well as the relationship of the text to music and movement, Arleo concludes that the "Susie" rhyme has spread from one country to another because it introduces the universal themes of courtship, marriage, motherhood, and death in a lighthearted, entertaining way. Although the rhyme seems long and complex, it is based on "simple repetitive structures, which emphasize the parallelism between text and music" (130). Arleo calls for a broader study of the Susie saga that includes other cultures and languages. He also suggests that children's folklore research would benefit from further research that "adopts an international perspective, in which performance analysis, focusing on the interactions among text, music and movement, is combined with cross-cultural and cross-linguistic comparison" (130).

Heather Russell's study "Play and Friendships in a Multi-Cultural Playground" (1986) examines games, verbal lore, informal activities, and friendship patterns of ethnically diverse children at Hightown Primary School in Melbourne. Russell asks important questions: "What are the dominant features of playground culture in a multi-cultural environment? Are there cross-cultural influences in games in the multi-cultural playground? Are there conflicts which arise from inter-ethnic tensions, and how are these dealt with? What are the play traditions of children from different ethnic backgrounds?" (2). Her answers to these questions reveal the complexity of playground culture.

Some playground games at Hightown "belong" to certain ethnic groups. High-Jump, for example, belongs to Chinese and Vietnamese children. While Elastics (jump rope) belongs to everyone, its most skilled and enthusiastic players are Chinese and Vietnamese girls (24). Russell notes that children playing marbles at Hightown accept two styles for shooting: the "Australian" and the "Chinese" style. Since the Chinese style does not come up in Dorothy Howard's study of Australian children's games or in other more recent collections, it seems that this shooting style has come to Australian playgrounds from Indo-Asian children's play relatively recently (27). Russell's study suggests that children of different ethnic backgrounds "should be encouraged to engage in folkloric play" and that teachers should allow children to choose their own play activities during lunchtime and recess (48–49).

Kathryn Marsh's essay "It's Not All Black or White: The Influence of the Media, the Classroom and Immigrant Groups on Children's Playground Singing Games" also examines folklore from a primary school in Australia. On this school's playground, where teachers encouraged the children to share games from their own ethnic backgrounds, Marsh recorded a number of interesting interactions, including simultaneous performances of "When Susie Was a Baby" and a performance of Scissors, Paper, Rock in both Korean and English. She concludes that teaching strategies in support of intercultural exchange help children from diverse backgrounds adjust to life at school and find acceptance from their peers. It is encouraging to hear that this kind of playground interaction "enables children to ensure that their play traditions will continue to flourish, despite the dire predictions of adults to the contrary" (94).

AGGRESSION AND VIOLENCE

It is necessary to distinguish between mock-violent and violent behavior. In her essay "'Sui Generis': Mock Violence in an Urban School Yard" (1996), Ann Richman Beresin explains that mock-violent games include games of playful fighting, wrestling, tagging, and ball playing. At the racially integrated public elementary school in Philadelphia where Beresin did her fieldwork, fourth- and fifth-graders loved to play Suicide or Sui, a handball game that involved running fast to avoid being hit by a tennis ball. Players who got hit by the ball three times had to go into the "tunnel," where other players could slam them with a ball. Beresin notes that Sui constitutes "a mixed genre, a 'double-voiced' form that is both ball game and a death drama, school yard game and institutional game" (33). Her analysis reminds us to avoid simplistic classification, as "mock violent games are one and many genres simultaneously" (33).

In schools and on playgrounds, bullying has caused severe anxiety for children and their teachers. Heather Russell's "Play and Friendships in a Multi-Cultural Playground" (1986) includes reflections on the "darker" side of playground life and lore: fights and intimidation of some children by others. Observing children's play at Hightown Primary School, Russell found that the school bully, a boy in grade six, "controlled, by way of force and intimidation, the activity of the upper grade boys" (83). When children told her a fight was about to happen, Russell felt compelled to intervene to protect the children. Her role as a stopper of fights became problematic; she worried that some children might view her as the bully's enemy and that the bully might punish "squealers" who told her that he was starting a fight. She stopped intervening in fights unless intervention was absolutely necessary and identified herself as the "games lady" (84).

Young people's assaults with guns have had tragic consequences. On April 20, 1999, two male adolescents killed 13 people at Columbine High School in Littleton, Colorado, and then killed themselves. This horrifying massacre elicited commentaries from people around the world, including concerned folklorists. In 2002 the *Children's Folklore Review* published a special issue on the Columbine massacre and adolescence. Examining both folk traditions and popular culture, the authors of essays in this special issue express significant insights related to adolescents' needs and cultural patterns. Bill Ellis's "Hitler's Birthday: Rumor-Panics in the Wake of the Columbine Shootings" puts rumor-panics following the Columbine massacre in historical and cultural context. Citing similar but less widely known rumor-panics that occurred in 1987 and 1989, Ellis analyzes them as "an emergent form of folk narrative" (23). JoAnn Conrad's "The War on Youth: A Modern Oedipal Tragedy" examines representations of youth as "the object of adult violence and rage, the object of adult moralistic anti-violence campaigns (violently implemented), and the object of adult desires" (39). Within the culture of high schools, certain behavior patterns contribute to outbreaks of violence. Allen Berres's "'Everybody Is Their Enemy': Goths, Spooky Kids, and the American School Shooting Panic" closely examines Columbine High School's "Trench Coat Mafia" and other rebellious groups of adolescents. Recognizing the "environment of fear" engendered by school shootings and subsequent lawsuits, Berres suggests that adults will continue to worry as long as groups or cliques of adolescents resist societal control (52).

After terrorists' attacks on the United States on September 11, 2001, children's play and games reflected Americans' struggle to come to terms with what had happened. Ann Richman Beresin's "Children's Expressive Culture in Light of September 11, 2001" perceptively analyzes how children played in Philadelphia shortly after the attacks occurred. Explaining that children's folklore has "always served as a window into the anxieties and ambivalence concerning specific wars and tragedies," Beresin discusses examples of post–September 11 play (331). Most of these forms of play build on traditional patterns. Four children, for example, make weapons out of iced-tea containers and pebbles. Forming two teams to shoot pebbles at each other, they call one team "Americans" and the other "Terrorists" (333). A little boy playing blocks crashes a wooden block "missile" into tall "buildings" that he has built. Seven- and nine-year-old boys give the nursery rhyme "London Bridge Is Falling Down" new words:

World TRADE Center is FALLING DOWN
FALLING DOWN, FALLING DOWN
World TRADE Center is FALLING DOWN
Oh—ON TOP of US. (331)

Beresin argues that educators should recognize the importance of such creative, open-ended play, which cannot happen at school unless time is allotted for recess. Her examples of children's play after September 11 support her contention that "the boundary between the rational and irrational is finer than we often acknowledge, that violence has its rationale for those who perpetuate it, and that children's irrational play indeed makes a lot of sense" (335). She also makes the interesting point that "cultures linked by hatred and cultures linked by play" converge at times of trauma (335).

In the years since the Columbine High School massacre and the September 11 terrorist attacks, some adults have viewed certain kinds of children's and adolescents' folklore as sources of danger. My article "'Mean Girls': The Reclassification of Children's and Adolescents' Folklore" (2002–03) gives examples of American school administrators' prohibition of such forms of children's folklore as slam books, pranks, insults, and graffiti. Since the fall of 2001, pranks involving fake bombs in middle schools and high schools have resulted in severe penalties, including expulsion from school and jail sentences. A *New York Times Magazine* article by Margaret Talbot, "Girls Just Want to Be Mean" (2002), brought the public's attention to girls' exclusion rituals that resulted in school administrators' hiring of professional intervention specialists. Soon afterwards, a number of books on girls' traditional behavior, including Rosalind Wiseman's *Queen Bees and Wannabes* (2002), became popular among parents and teachers.

Since children's folklore scholars understand the dynamics of children's play and games, they can interpret the meaning of children's expressive behavior during difficult times. Knowing how children tend to respond to crises, they can reassure concerned adults that reactive play gives children an important opportunity to express themselves. In *The People in the Playground* (1993), Iona Opie invites readers to enjoy the "defiant light-heartedness" of children's play. With refreshing insight, she observes, "The children are clowning. They are making fun of life; and if an enquiring adult becomes too serious about words and rules they say: 'It's only a game, isn't it? It's just for fun. *I* don't know what it means. It doesn't *matter*'" (15).

WORKS CITED

Abrahams, Roger. "Introductory Remarks to a Rhetorical Theory of Folklore." *Journal of American Folklore* 81.320 (1968): 143–58.

Arleo, Andy. "The Saga of Susie: The Dynamics of an International Handclapping Game." *Play Today in the Primary School Playground.* Ed. Julia C. Bishop and Mavis Curtis. Buckingham, Eng., and Philadelphia: Open UP, 2001. 115–32.

Armitage, Marc. "The Ins and Outs of School Playground Play: Children's Use of 'Play Places.'" *Play Today in the Primary School Playground.* Ed. Julia C. Bishop and Mavis Curtis. Buckingham, Eng., and Philadelphia: Open UP, 2001. 37–58.

Bauman, Richard. "Ethnography of Children's Folklore." *Children In and Out of School: Ethnography and Education.* Ed. Perry Gilmore and Allan A. Glatthorn. Washington, DC: Center for Applied Linguistics, 1982. 172–87.

Ben-Amos, Dan. "Toward a Definition of Folklore in Context." *Journal of American Folklore* 84.331 (1971): 3–15.

Beresin, Ann Richman. "Children's Expressive Culture in Light of September 11, 2001." *Anthropology and Education Quarterly* 33.3 (2002): 331–37.

———. "'Sui Generis': Mock Violence in an Urban School Yard." *Children's Folklore Review* 18.2 (1996): 25–35.

Berres, Allen. "'Everybody Is Their Enemy': Goths, Spooky Kids, and the American School Shooting Panic." *Children's Folklore Review* 24 (2002): 43–54.

Blackman, Shane J. "'Poxy Cupid!' An Ethnographic and Feminist Account of a Resistant Female Youth Culture: The New Wave Girls." *Cool Places: Geographies of Youth Cultures.* Ed. Tracey Skelton and Gill Valentine. London and New York: Routledge, 1998. 207–28.

Boyes, Georgina. "Alice Bertha Gomme (1852–1938): A Reassessment of the Work of a Folklorist." *Folklore* 101.2 (1990): 198–208.

Brady, Margaret K. *"Some Kind of Power": Navajo Children's Skinwalker Narratives.* Salt Lake City: U of Utah P, 1984.

Bronner, Simon J. *American Children's Folklore.* Little Rock: August, 1988.

Chambers, Robert. *Select Writings of Robert Chambers: Popular Rhymes of Scotland.* 1826. Whitefish, MT: Kessinger, 2007.

Conrad, JoAnn. "The War on Youth: A Modern Oedipal Tragedy." *Children's Folklore Review* 24.1–2 (2002): 33–42.

Cott, Jonathan. "Profiles: Finding Out Is Better." *New Yorker.* April 4, 1983: 47–91.

Darian-Smith, Kate, and June Factor, eds. *Child's Play: Dorothy Howard and the Folklore of Australian Children.* Melbourne: Museum Victoria, 2005.

Dégh, Linda. *Legend and Belief.* Bloomington: Indiana UP, 2001.

Dorson, Richard M. *The British Folklorists: A History.* Chicago: U of Chicago P, 1968.

Dundes, Alan. "Bloody Mary in the Mirror." *Bloody Mary in the Mirror: Essays in Psychoanalytic Folkloristics.* Jackson: UP of Mississippi, 2002. 76–94.

———. "The Dead Baby Joke Cycle." *Western Folklore* 38.3 (1979): 145–57.

———. "On the Psychology of Legend." *American Folk Legend: A Symposium.* Ed. Wayland D. Hand. Berkeley: U of California P, 1971. 21–36.

Eifermann, Rivka R. "Social Play in Childhood." *Child's Play.* Ed. R. E. Herron and Brian Sutton-Smith. New York: Wiley, 1971. 270–309.

Ellis, Bill. *Aliens, Ghosts, and Cults: Legends We Live.* Jackson: UP of Mississippi, 2003.

———. "Hitler's Birthday: Rumor-Panics in the Wake of the Columbine Shootings." *Children's Folklore Review* 24 (2002): 21–32.

———. *Lucifer Ascending: The Occult in Folklore and Popular Culture.* Lexington: UP of Kentucky, 2004.

———. *Raising the Devil.* Lexington: UP of Kentucky, 2000.

Fine, Gary Alan. "Rude Words: Insults and Narration in Preadolescent Obscene Talk." *Maledicta* 5 (1981): 51–68.

Freud, Sigmund. "The Acquisition and Control of Fire." 1932. *Psychoanalytic Electronic Publishing.* 2008. http://www.pep-web.org/document.php?id=SE.022.0183A.

Goldstein, Kenneth S. "Strategy in Counting-Out: An Ethnographic Field Study." *The Study of Games.* Ed. Elliott M. Avedon and Brian Sutton-Smith. New York: Wiley, 1971. 167–78.

Gomme, Alice Bertha. *The Traditional Games of England, Scotland, and Ireland.* 2 vols. 1894–98. New York: Dover, 1964.

Goodwin, Marjorie Harness. "The Serious Side of Jump Rope: Conversational Practices and Social Organization in the Frame of Play." *Journal of American Folklore* 98.389 (1985): 315–30.

Grider, Sylvia. "The Haunted House in Literature, Popular Culture, and Tradition: A Consistent Image." *Contemporary Legend* new series 2 (1999): 174–204.

Grugeon, Elizabeth. "'We Like Singing the Spice Girl Songs...and We Like Tig and Stuck in the Mud': Girls' Traditional Games in Two Playgrounds." *Play Today in the Primary School Playground.* Ed. Julia C. Bishop and Mavis Curtis. Buckingham, Eng., and Philadelphia: Open UP, 2001. 98–114.

Halliwell, James O. *The Nursery Rhymes of England.* London: Percy Society, 1842.

———. *Popular Rhymes and Nursery Tales of England.* 1849. London: Bodley Head, 1970.

Hart, Roger. *Children's Experience of Place.* New York: Irvington, 1979.

Howard, Dorothy G. M. "Folk Jingles of American Children." Dissertation, New York University, 1938.

———. "Introduction to Dover Edition." *The Traditional Games of England, Scotland, and Ireland.* By Alice Bertha Gomme. Vol. 1. New York: Dover, 1964. v–xvi.

———. "Post Script, 1990" to "Folk Jingles of American Children: A Collection and Study of Rhymes Used by Children Today." Quoted in June Factor, "A Forgotten Pioneer." *Child's Play: Dorothy Howard and the Folklore of Australian Children.* Ed. Kate Darian-Smith and June Factor. Melbourne: Museum Victoria, 2005. 1–18.

Hughes, Linda A. "'You Have to Do It with Style': Girls' Games and Girls' Gaming." *Feminist Theory and the Study of Folklore.* Ed. Susan Tower Hollis, Linda Pershing, and M. Jane Young. Urbana: U of Illinois P, 1993. 130–48.

Jorgensen, Marilyn G. "An Analysis of Boy-Girl Relationships Portrayed in Contemporary Jump Rope and Handclapping Rhymes." *Southwest Folklore* 4.3–4 (1980): 63–71.

Kelsey, Nigel. "Norman Douglas Revisited." *London Lore* 1.10 (October 1983): 117–25.

Klintberg, Bengt af. "'Black Madame, Come Out!': On Schoolchildren and Spirits." *Arv* 44 (1988): 155–67.

Knapp, Mary, and Herbert Knapp. *One Potato, Two Potato: The Secret Education of American Children.* New York: Norton, 1976.

Langlois, Janet. "'Mary Whales, I Believe in You': Myth and Ritual Subdued." *Indiana Folklore* 11.1 (1978): 5–33.

Legman, Gershon. *Rationale of the Dirty Joke.* New York: Grove, 1968.

Lüthi, Max. *Once Upon a Time: On the Nature of Fairy Tales.* Bloomington: Indiana UP, 1976.

Marsh, Kathryn. "It's Not All Black or White: The Influence of the Media, the Classroom, and Immigrant Groups on Children's Playground Singing Games." *Play Today in the Primary School Playground.* Ed. Julia C. Bishop and Mavis Curtis. Buckingham, Eng., and Philadelphia: Open UP, 2001. 80–97.

McDowell, John H. "The Speech Play and Verbal Art of Chicano Children: An Ethnographic and Sociolinguistic Study." Diss., U of Texas at Austin, 1975.

Mechling, Jay. "The Magic of the Boy Scout Campfire." *Journal of American Folklore* 93 (1980): 35–56.

Mergen, Bernard. "Children's Lore in School and Playgrounds." *Children's Folklore: A Source Book.* Ed. Brian Sutton-Smith, Jay Mechling, Thomas W. Johnson, and Felicia R. McMahon. New York and London: Garland, 1995. 229–50.

Newell, William Wells. *Games and Songs of American Children.* 1883. New York: Dover, 1963.

Opie, Iona. *The People in the Playground.* New York: Oxford UP, 1993.

Opie, Iona, and Peter Opie. *Children's Games in Street and Playground.* New York: Oxford UP, 1969.

————. *I Saw Esau: Traditional Rhymes of Youth.* London: Williams and Norgate, 1947.

————. *The Lore and Language of Schoolchildren.* New York: Oxford UP, 1959.

————. *The Oxford Dictionary of Nursery Rhymes.* 1951. Oxford: Clarendon, 1973.

————. *The Singing Game.* New York: Oxford UP, 1985.

Piaget, Jean. *The Moral Judgment of the Child.* 1932. New York: Free, 1965.

Riley, Linda. "Extremes: How Girls Play Slaughter, How Boys Play Slaughter at Valley Oak Elementary." *Children's Folklore Review* 13.1 (1990): 10–16.

Roemer, Danielle M. "A Social Interactional Analysis of Anglo Children's Folklore: Catches and Narratives." Diss., U of Texas at Austin, 1977.

Russell, Heather. *Play and Friendships in a Multi-Cultural Playground.* Melbourne: Australian Children's Folklore Publications, 1986.

Strutt, Joseph. *Sports and Pastimes of the People of England.* London: Tegg, 1801.

Sutton-Smith, Brian. *The Ambiguity of Play.* Cambridge: Harvard UP, 1998.

————. "Courage in the Playground: A Tribute to Dorothy Howard." *Child's Play: Dorothy Howard and the Folklore of Australian Children.* Ed. Kate Darian-Smith and June Factor. Melbourne: Museum Victoria, 2005. 187–204.

————. *The Folkgames of Children.* Austin: U of Texas P, 1972.

————. *The Folkstories of Children.* Philadelphia: U of Pennsylvania P, 1981.

————. *The Games of New Zealand Children.* Los Angeles and Berkeley: U of California P, 1959.

————. *A History of Children's Play: The New Zealand Playground 1840–1950.* Philadelphia: U of Pennsylvania P, 1981.

————. "A Play Biography." *Children's Folklore Review* 20.1–2 (1997–98): 5–42.

————. "The Play of Girls." *Becoming Female.* Ed. Claire B. Kopp and Martha Kirkpatrick. New York: Plenum, 1979. 229–57.

Talbot, Margaret, "Girls Just Want to Be Mean." *The New York Times Magazine* (February 24, 2002): 24–65.

Tucker, Elizabeth. "Concepts of Space in Children's Narratives." *Folklore on Two Continents: Essays in Honor of Linda Dégh.* Ed. Nikolai Burlakoff and Carl Lindahl. Bloomington: Trickster, 1980. 19–25.

————. "Ghosts in Mirrors: Reflections of the Self." *Journal of American Folklore* 118.468 (2005): 186–203.

————. "Levitation and Trance Sessions at Preadolescent Girls' Slumber Parties." *The Masks of Play.* Ed. Brian Sutton-Smith and Diana Kelly-Byrne. New York: Leisure, 1984. 125–33.

————. "'Mean Girls': The Reclassification of Children's and Adolescents' Folklore." *Children's Folklore Review* 25.1–2 (2002–03): 7–22.

Van Rheenan, Derek. "Boys Who Play Hopscotch: The Historical Divide of a Gendered Space." *Children's Folklore Review* 21.1 (1998): 5–34.

Virtanen, Leea. *Children's Lore.* Studia Fennica 22. Helsinki: Suomalisen Kirjallisuuden Seura, 1978.

Wiltshire, Robin. "The Nigel Kelsey Collection of Folklore, 1962–1990." *Folklore* 112.1 (April 2001): 82–87.

Wiseman, Rosalind. *Queen Bees and Wannabes: Helping Your Daughter Survive Cliques, Gossip, Boyfriends, and Other Realities of Adolescence.* New York: Crown, 2002.

Withers, Carl. "Introduction to Dover Edition." *Games and Songs of American Children.* By William Wells Newell. New York: Dover, 1963.

Wolfenstein, Martha. *Children's Humor: A Psychological Analysis.* New York: Free, 1954. Bloomington: Indiana UP, 1978.

Zumwalt, Rosemary. "Plain and Fancy: A Content Analysis of Children's Jokes Dealing with Adult Sexuality." *Readings in American Folklore.* Ed. Jan Harold Brunvand. New York: Norton, 1979. 345–54.

Five

Contexts

AUTOBIOGRAPHY

Many autobiographies include details from the author's childhood years. These publications offer perceptions of children's folklore in its familial and cultural context. Bernard Mergen's examination of autobiographies from the seventeenth century to the early 1980s resulted in important insights regarding children's play and use of toys (186–90). Study of autobiographies helps us understand how children interact with other people and material objects at home, at school, and elsewhere.

One of the most detailed and insightful recollections of childhood is Dorothy Mills Howard's *Dorothy's World: Childhood in Sabine Bottom, 1902–1910* (1977). Having studied childlore in Australia as well as the United States and Mexico, Howard understood the traditional patterns of her own early years in Texas. Her book includes a chapter for each year from birth to "seven going on eight," as well as chapters devoted to her home, her family's farm, clothes for everyday life and special occasions, play life, and songs. Her long lists of games and songs demonstrate the richness of folk tradition in Texas during the first decade of the twentieth century.

At the age of four, Dorothy Gray Mills learned to write her name backwards: "Sllim Yarg Ythorod." When her sisters teased her by calling her "Old Gray Mule," she told them that her new name was a secret between herself and her grandmother (63). Howard enjoyed many kinds of play and games, from making an indoor or outdoor playhouse to staging funerals for pets and dolls, playing the circle game Frog in the Middle, rolling hoops, jumping rope, walking on stilts, bouncing up and down on a seesaw, and playing Thimble, Thimble on cold, rainy days. Most toys were homemade; very few came from the revered Sears and Roebuck mail-order catalog. Howard's memoir gives the reader a satisfying glimpse of childlore in its proper context of family, community, and folk belief.

Other insights come from the autobiography of African American folklorist Zora Neale Hurston, who was born in Eatonville, Florida, in 1891. At an early age, Hurston learned how boys' play differed from girls' play:

> I discovered that I was extra strong by playing with other girls near my age. I had no way of judging the force of my playful blows, and so I was always hurting somebody. Then they would say I meant to hurt, and go home and leave me. Everything was all right, however, when I played with boys. It was a shameful thing to admit being hurt among them. Furthermore, they could dish it out themselves, and I was acceptable to them because I was the one girl who could take a good pummeling without running home to tell. (39)

Hurston's family put a stop to this rough play, believing that it was "not ladylike." Thwarted in her play preferences, Hurston, "driven inward," developed an interest in telling and listening to stories (40).

C. S. Lewis, author of *Surprised by Joy,* also experienced disappointments. Wynyard School, which Lewis entered after the death of his mother in 1908, allowed bullying, but Lewis's older brother protected him. Malvern College, which Lewis entered in 1913, allowed older boys, called "Bloods," to give younger "fags" long lists of tasks to complete each day. Even though the school paid people to shine the boys' shoes, older boys forced younger ones to keep their shoes spotless and to perform other menial tasks (96). Lewis found the school's status system so disturbing that he begged his father for permission to leave school and continue studying with a private tutor. Fortunately, his father allowed Lewis to leave, and the rest of his school days passed pleasantly.

More jocular memoirs describe pranks. Frank B. Gilbreth Jr.'s book *Cheaper by the Dozen* (1948) describes a family of 12 children growing up in the early twentieth century. Frank B. Gilbreth Sr., the children's father, played the part of a prankster by asking each of his children, in turn, to look for the "birdie" inside the engine of the family's new car. While the child waited, the father blew the car's horn loudly. Bill, Frank Jr.'s younger brother, impulsively decided to play the same prank while his father had his head inside the car's hood after a breakdown. When the horn suddenly sounded, Frank Sr. jumped, striking his head against the car's hood and burning his wrist against the engine's exhaust pipe. Later, after recovering from the shock of the unexpected prank, he enjoyed telling others "the story about Bill and the birdie" (15), which demonstrated his son's prowess as a prankster.

Pranks and other kinds of children's folklore emerge in the remarkable autobiography *They Called Me Mayer July: Painted Memories of a Jewish Childhood in Poland before the Holocaust* (2007), by Mayer Kirshenblatt and Barbara

Kirshenblatt-Gimblett. During his early years in the village of Apt, Mayer Kirshenblatt played pranks on girls. One day he and his friends covered themselves in white wrapping paper from a grocery store and stood on their school's steps, pretending to be ghosts. Girls ran away from them, shouting "Demons! Demons!" (265). Kirshenblatt also enjoyed playing a prank practiced by Polish schoolboys for generations: gluing their teacher's beard to the table with melted candle wax.

Although children in the village of Apt spent many hours in school during the 1920s and 1930s, they enjoyed a rich and varied set of games. Kirshenblatt explains, "Mostly, we made our own fun" (307). Boys' games included *palant* (a game similar to baseball, played with two sticks and two rocks) and *fusbal* (soccer). Girls played jacks with neck bones of geese that had been boiled to remove all the flesh. During Passover, children played nut games similar to games played with marbles. Among the delights of summertime were fly and snail races. Children recited traditional rhymes to tease snails out of their shells, including "Snail, snail, show us your horns. We will give you bread on the floor" (291). They also enjoyed making toys, including bows, arrows, guns, willow whips, and two kinds of slingshots.

Another intriguing autobiography of a European childhood is *The Wheel of Life: A Memoir of Living and Dying* (1997) by Dr. Elisabeth Kübler-Ross, founder of the contemporary hospice movement. Born a triplet in Switzerland in 1926, Kübler-Ross shared a room with her sisters Eva and Erika, whose beds, chairs, and clothes were identical to her own. Although she spent many hours playing with her sisters, Kübler-Ross wanted to find a way of life that differentiated her from the rest of her family. Being a sensitive and affectionate child, she did her best to help others. At school, she energetically protected children tormented by bullies:

My fists pummeled the backs of the school's bullies so often that my mother was accustomed to the butcher boy, the town gossip, passing by our house after class and saying, "Betli will be late today. She's beating up one of the boys." My parents never got mad, since they knew I only protected those who could not defend themselves. (35)

Since Kübler-Ross became a physician who devoted herself to patients struggling with serious illness, these antibullying incidents foreshadowed her future career.

Other recollections of childhood emphasize imaginative play. The Chilean author Isabel Allende, born in 1942, lived with her grandparents in Lima, Peru. Her favorite place was the cellar, where she "used to read by candlelight, dream of magic castles, dress up like a ghost, invent black masses, build forts out of an entire series of books that one of [her] uncles wrote about India, and then fall asleep among the spiders and mice." The richness of Allende's solitary play gave her immense satisfaction. Because the cellar was "a beautiful world where the imagination knew no limits," it nurtured her development as a teller and writer of stories (Rodden 54).

Comparable reflections about mid-twentieth-century childhood in the United States appear in Hillary Rodham Clinton's "An Idyllic Childhood" (2001) and *Living History* (2003). As a small child in Park Ridge, Illinois, Clinton designed a spaceship in the basement of her family's house. Her two-year-old brother Hugh came along with her on "space trips," sometimes hearing bad news from his older sister. Clinton explains, "To this day he says he was warped for life because one time I threw him out of the space ship and left him floating in space, and told him he couldn't come up to lunch because he was lost somewhere around Mercury" ("Idyllic" 164). With her mother, Clinton built a "fantasy world in a large cardboard box" and made up stories for which her dolls became characters (*Living History* 10).

Clinton also spent many hours playing "chase and run," a game in which team members ran toward safe areas within a two- or three-block section of their neighborhood. Summer pursuits included corner baseball, softball, and kickball, with sewer lids as bases. Clinton enjoyed active sports, including backyard hockey and neighborhood Olympics. She expresses sadness about twenty-first-century American children having less unsupervised playtime and hopes that their time for play and games will increase: "That would be one of the best gifts we could give our children" (165).

Another contemporary memoir that eloquently describes the importance of creative play is Jeannette Walls's *The Glass Castle* (2005). Walls's brilliant, eccentric father and free-spirited, artistic mother gave their children love and encouragement but often let the children go hungry as the family moved from one place to another. Money was scarce, and the children slept in cardboard boxes when they were small; once they were old enough to go to school, Walls and her sisters and brother foraged in garbage cans for leftover food from other children's lunches. One memorable Christmas, when her father could not afford to buy any presents, he gave each of his children a wonderful gift: the choice of a star in the desert sky. With very few restrictions on playtime activities, the Walls children looked for treasures at the town dump, played with matches, and mixed several kinds of hazardous waste to create what they called "nuclear fuel" (61). They also spent time playing Red Rover, Red Light Green Light, and other traditional games with neighborhood kids. Stamina came from playing "nameless games that involved running hard, keeping up with the pack, and not crying if you fell down" (58).

At school, the Walls children endured other children's taunts and assaults. When the bully Ernie Goad told the Walls kids, "Y'all are a bunch of garbage," they retaliated by making a catapult with ropes, a mattress, and rocks. Hurling "an arsenal of rocks" at Ernie and his gang, the Walls kids triumphantly drove their tormenters away (165–67). Later, during sixth grade, Jeannette's classmates called her "spider legs, skeleton girl, pipe cleaner, two-by-four, bony butt, stick woman, bean pole, and giraffe"; they also told her she could keep dry during a thunderstorm if she stood under a telephone wire (173). In spite of these insults, she found her niche at school as a journalist and gained respect as a serious writer.

Pascal Khoo Thwe, the author of *From the Land of Green Ghosts: A Burmese Odyssey* (2002), was born in Burma in 1967. A member of the Padaung people, Thwe enjoyed a childhood influenced by folk beliefs and traditions. A few weeks after his birth, his father rubbed a pulverized spider on his head to make him smart and hardworking. His grandmother, who had traveled to England as a member of Bertram Mills's circus, spat on his head three times to save him from evil spirits. As a young child, Thwe slept in a big bed with his parents and siblings, surrounded by the comforting sounds and smells of his family group.

At the age of five, Thwe reluctantly left home to attend a government boarding school. His teacher, Mr. Joseph, bullied his pupils, and the children bullied each other:

They carried catapults, flint pellets, knives and other ingeniously painful homemade weapons. I was a new target, and it seemed impossible not to be part of the system of bullying. Not only did they bully you, they also forced you to join them in bullying others, to cheat in exams and even to ambush unsuspecting teachers on their way home. To hurt me they would call me by my father's name, because for some reason we Padaung found it insulting when someone uttered the names of our parents. (45–46)

Thwe's helplessness as a victim of bullying mirrors many other children's feelings in similar situations. Fortunately, after Thwe told his Uncle Yew about the problem, Uncle Yew started spending time at the government school, taking the children on hunting expeditions, and showing them how to practice better behavior.

Thwe's autobiography also includes other kinds of childhood folklore. He and his friends chased each other, "jumping from branch to branch like monkeys" (74). Spending nights in his own tree house, he watched the stars until he fell asleep; some of his dreams became predictions of future events that his family took very seriously. Eventually, he became the "unofficial family oracle" (53). Belief in ghosts enlivened his childhood years. As a small boy, he worried about going outside to the bathroom near the parish priest's house, which had a reputation for being haunted. If the priest found excrement near his house, he made children walk around it until one of the children admitted who had defecated on the ground (27). Besides worrying about the haunted area near the priest's house, Thwe and his friends feared "green ghosts," the vengeful spirits of people who had died because of accident or murder (85). Ghosts continued to be important presences throughout his college years, when he shared a dwelling with other students and became a guerrilla fighter against the government's forces.

CHILDREN'S LITERATURE

The first printed book for children, John Newbery's *A Little Pretty Pocket-Book, Intended for the Instruction and Amusement of Little Master Tommy and Pretty Miss Polly,* was published in England in 1744. Combining alphabet letters with morally uplifting verses and entertaining illustrations, Newbery's book succeeded in pleasing young readers. Each copy was sold with a ball and a pincushion; following eighteenth-century gender roles, the ball was for boys, while the pincushion was for girls. The *Little Pretty Pocket-Book*'s illustrations help folklorists understand patterns of eighteenth-century British children's play. Its description of "base-ball" is the first reference to that game in print. Besides offering information about what children enjoyed doing then, the book demonstrates its author's belief in combining useful lessons with amusement.

During the nineteenth century, books of fantasy and realistic fiction for children became popular. Lewis Carroll's *Alice's Adventures in Wonderland* (1865) delighted children and adults with its imaginative portrayal of a little girl entering a secondary world through a rabbit hole. *Through the Looking Glass* (1871) further developed Alice's adventures. The first of these two fantasy classics shows the influence of children's folklore, including riddles, puns, and nonsense rhymes. "Jabberwocky," a poem based on nonsense words, has become one of the best-known poems in English literature. Another amusing piece of verse is "Twinkle, Twinkle, Little Bat," a parody of the popular children's song "Twinkle, Twinkle, Little Star."

Mid-nineteenth-century realistic fiction for children reflects the gender roles of that era. In Louisa May Alcott's *Little Women* (1867), the four March sisters play games together, act out dramas for their family, and dream about the future. Most of their activity takes place inside the domestic sphere of their family's home. In contrast to Alcott's four female characters, the protagonist of Mark Twain's *The Adventures of Tom Sawyer* (1871) skips school, goes swimming, explores a cave, plays pranks on his friends, and fakes his own funeral. Both Tom Sawyer and the March sisters enjoy traditional amusements that were common during that time period.

In the early twentieth century, the American "Our Little Cousin" series attempted to teach young readers about the games and customs of children living in other parts of the world. Blanche McManus's *Our Little Scotch Cousin* (1906), for example, explains that on Saint Patrick's Day, Scottish boys wearing blue ribbons fight with Irish boys wearing green ribbons. On Halloween, Scottish children play "queer games" and eat pieces of a cake into which a silver coin has been inserted. Instead of promoting understanding of other cultures, the book focuses on quaint deviation from familiar customs. Similarly, Mary Hazleton Wade's *Our Little Indian Cousin* (1901) introduces a boy named Yellow Thunder, whose family drinks a "queer drink" and celebrates perplexing holidays. "How you would laugh to see them gathering at a party," the author tells her young readers (70). The only neutral description is a matter-of-fact explanation of how children play lacrosse (67).

Some children's books of the early twentieth century combine adventures in mysterious places with guidelines for a happy, healthful life. In Frances Hodgson Burnett's novel *The Secret Garden* (1909), Mary Lennox, a fretful child whose parents have died in India, goes to England to live in her uncle's mansion on a Yorkshire moor. After receiving a skipping rope from her nursery maid, Mary discovers the delights of outdoor play. She finds the key to an abandoned garden and learns how exciting it can be to bring a garden back to life. Her invalid cousin Colin joins her in the secret garden and eventually learns to walk there. Fresh air, healthful exercise, and rituals derived from Mary's knowledge of East Indian fakirs give both children better health and hope for the future.

Boy blows bubbles at a high school graduation party in the summer of 2007 in New York. Photograph by Geoffrey Gould.

In the 1930s, historical novels about pioneer families' adventures became popular in the United States. Laura Ingalls Wilder's *Little House in the Big Woods* (1932) includes details of rural Wisconsin children's amusements, such as a balloon game played with the blown-up bladder of a slaughtered pig. *Little House on the Prairie* (1935) explains how the children kept busy while their family traveled west to Kansas in a covered wagon. Similarly, Carol Ryrie Brink's *Caddie Woodlawn* (1935), based on a grandmother's oral narratives about growing up on the Wisconsin frontier, describes traditional games, pastimes, and pranks.

Children's traditions also appear in J.R.R. Tolkien's *The Hobbit* (1938). Bilbo Baggins, the book's small, childlike hero, loves to eat and attend birthday parties. Against his will, Bilbo joins a group of elves and dwarves on a quest to kill a dragon. He finds a ring that makes him invisible and uses the ring as the subject of a neck riddle, which saves him from being gobbled up by the evil Gollum. Other riddles posed by both Bilbo and Gollum give the reader a sense of the richness of British oral tradition.

In 1949, Brian Sutton-Smith published realistic fiction for children in New Zealand. Having grown up in the city of Wellington, Sutton-Smith knew that schoolchildren would respond well to descriptions of daily life similar to their own. He wrote about "the ordinary play and misdemeanors of four boys, sitting in the sun discussing their choices for play, or playing rugby and cricket in the street, hitting balls through windows and sneaking into the flicks (movies) for free, being carelessly destructive at birthday parties, digging to make underground forts and coming up with dog bones" ("Play Biography" 7). Sutton-Smith's stories encouraged children to write essays of their own; they also made the author "think more extensively about [his] own childhood past" (11).

One of the most beloved American authors of realistic fiction for children is Beverly Cleary, whose books *Henry Huggins* (1950) and *Beezus and Ramona* (1955) depict children's daily activities with gentle humor. Henry adopts a dog, raises gallons of guppies, and tries to save money. In *Henry and the Clubhouse* (1962), Henry and his friends build a simple shelter, making rules about who can and cannot come in. Henry's friend Beezus has a pesky but imaginative little sister, Ramona, whose shenanigans fill a series of books culminating in *Ramona Forever* (1984). As a young child, Ramona walks on tin-can stilts and plays Brick Factory with her friend Howie. When she goes to school, she plays playground games and exchanges friendly insults with other children. Cleary's books about Ramona, Beezus, and Henry still please children of the twenty-first century.

Children's literature scholars tend to put realistic fiction and fantasy into separate categories, but many works of fantasy literature have a solid foundation in children's play and playground hierarchies. In C. S. Lewis's *The Silver Chair* (1953), for example, schoolchildren Eustace and Jill discuss bullies' torment behind their school's gym. Eustace asks, "Didn't I stand up to Carter about the rabbit? And didn't I keep the secret about Spivvins—under torture too?" (3). Asking Aslan, the great lion, to bring them from their school to the enchanted world of Narnia, Eustace and Jill gladly exchange their school's grim environs for the quest to save Prince Rilian from the clutches of an evil witch. When Eustace and Jill return to school, Aslan frightens the gang of bullies, whose names indicate their nastiness: "Edith Winterblott, 'Spotty' Sorner, big Bannister, and the two loathsome Garrett twins" (255). Aslan's visit scares the bullies and the school's headmistress so much that changes take place, and pupils at the school begin to enjoy a more peaceful, comfortable way of life.

In the early 1970s, realistic fiction for children began to include more material from the childhood underground. Judy Blume's controversial "young adult" novels quickly gained many young fans but shocked some parents and teachers. *Are You There, God? It's Me, Margaret* (1970) explores girls' beliefs and rituals related to menstruation and breast development, which had not previously appeared in children's literature. The counterpart of that book for boys on the verge of puberty is *Then Again, Maybe I Won't* (1971). *Blubber* (1974) looks at children's cruelty toward overweight classmates, and *Forever* (1975) describes a girl's decision to become sexually active. Through Blume's books, adults have gained a better sense of the dynamics of children's traditions.

In 1992 the Children's Folklore Section of the American Folklore Society first awarded its Aesop Prize and Aesop Accolades, which commend authors and illustrators for basing their work on folk tradition. The first winners of the Aesop Prize were Barbara Bader and Arthur Geisert's *Aesop and Company with Scenes from his Legendary Life* and Eric A. Kimmel and Erika Weihs's *Days of Awe: Stories for Rosh Hashanah and Yom Kippur*. Julie Hearn's *The Minister's Daughter*, which received an Aesop Accolade in 2005, is one of the recent winners that emphasizes children's folklore.

A new era of children's fantasy literature began when J. K. Rowling's *Harry Potter and the Sorcerer's Stone* was published in 1997. Harry Potter, an orphan who sleeps in a cupboard under a staircase, fits the characterization of unpromising folktale heroes. Once he enters Hogwarts Academy of Witchcraft and Wizardry, Harry makes new friends and gets acquainted with resident ghosts Nearly Headless Nick and Peeves the Poltergeist. He quickly becomes adept at quidditch, a ball game played by students flying on broomsticks. Learning a spell to make objects fly—"Wingardium Leviosa!"—Harry goes a step beyond the levitation ritual that children have practiced since the seventeenth century (170–71). As he gets accustomed to life at Hogwarts, Harry must confront the bullying of Draco Malfoy and his subservient friends. J. K. Rowling's understanding of the childhood underground substantially contributes to the appeal of her books, which have delighted children around the world.

FILM

School

A number of films about children and adolescents focus on troubles at school. Jean Vigo's *Zéro de Conduite* [Zero for Conduct] came out in 1933 and was banned in France until 1946. This innovative film, only 41 minutes long, depicts daily life at a repressive French boarding school for boys. Cruel teachers give the boys so many zeros for poor conduct that the boys rebel and take over the school. One of the film's most engaging scenes is the one in which the boys engage in a pillow fight, marching in slow motion through swirling feathers. This film about the childhood underground's victory became a model for future films, including François Truffaut's *Les Quatre Cents Coups* [The 400 Blows].

In England, *The Belles of St. Trinian's* (1954) set a pattern for humorous films about girls' schools: constant high jinks and rebellion in a large, venerable school building. The spirited St. Trinian's girls throw smoke bombs, burn down buildings, steal a racehorse, and fight with sticks and pillows. A later American film, *The Trouble with Angels* (1966), similarly highlights outrageous pranks. Mary (Hayley Mills) and her best friend Rachel (June Harding) respond to roll call with fake names, take fellow students on a tour of the nuns' cloister, fill sugar bowls with bubble bath, and blow such enormous smoke rings that a nun calls the fire department. The school's Mother Superior (Rosalind Russell) handles crises so well that Mary eventually decides to follow her example and become a nun. In the film's last scene Mary waves goodbye to her friends, perhaps anticipating poetic justice: students in her future classes playing pranks of their own.

The lighthearted comedy *Ferris Bueller's Day Off* (1986) portrays warfare between high school students and school administrators. Ferris (Matthew Broderick) is a teenage trickster hero. Although his elaborate pranks fool his parents and teachers, he cannot deceive his sister Jeanie (Jennifer Grey) or Dean Rooney (Jeffrey Jones), whose greatest desire is to make Ferris stay in high school for one more year. Through a clever set-up of electronic devices, Ferris convinces his parents that he is much too ill to go to school; then, with his best friends Cameron (Allan Ruck) and Sloane (Mia Sera), he drives off to the big city for a day of fun. After many high jinks, he makes it home just in time to greet his parents and foil Dean Rooney's plot to prove that he has been playing hooky. This subversive movie has become such a classic that it has engendered its own traditions, with lines of dialogue printed on T-shirts and recited at parties by teenage fans.

In the more serious film *Au Revoir les Enfants* [Goodbye, Children] (1987), directed by Louis Malle, boys at a Catholic boarding school in France during World War II suffer from the proximity of German soldiers. Julien Quentin (Gaspard Manesse), one of the school's most intelligent and sensitive students, becomes friends with a new student, Jean Bonnet (Raphaël Fejitö). After seeing

Jean perform a religious ritual with candles late at night, Julien realizes that his new friend is Jewish. Malle brilliantly juxtaposes play and games with scenes involving German soldiers. In one scene, boys on stilts try to knock each other down and shout insults at each other: "Lion heart! Pig face! Flea brain!" A longer segment of the film shows the boys playing Capture the Flag, playfully competing with each other while adults wage war. At the film's end, Gestapo officers capture Jean and two other boys. This sad, moving film reflects Malle's own experience as a child at school in France during World War II.

Some presentations of teenagers' troubles take the form of horror movies. In *The Craft* (1996), Sarah (Robin Tunney), who has just survived a suicide attempt, meets three black-garbed girls—Rochelle (Rachel True), Bonnie (Neve Campbell), and Nancy (Fairuza Balk)—at her new high school. Like the three witches in Shakespeare's *Macbeth,* these girls spend their free time together plotting malicious spells. After Sarah joins the group, the girls buy books of magic and cast spells to get revenge against a callous boy and a prejudiced girl. Eventually, their spells work; the boy falls hopelessly in love with Sarah, earning his friends' scorn, and the girl bursts into tears when she starts losing her beautiful blond hair. In one of the movie's most entertaining scenes, Sarah, Nancy, and Bonnie perform the ritual "Light As a Feather," trying to lift Rochelle with two fingers of each of their hands. Quickly and smoothly, Rochelle rises up into the air. After the girls remove their hands, she still floats in front of them. When Bonnie's mother opens the door, Rochelle falls to the floor. The alarmed mother shouts, "Are you girls getting high?" Of course Rochelle *has* been getting high, but not on drugs. This scene marks a turning point: playful magic becomes real.

Mean Girls (2004), a film about a difficult adjustment to a new school, asks an intriguing question: how can a teenage girl home-schooled by zoologist parents in East Africa adjust to daily life at a public high school in the United States? Cady, the 16-year-old central character and narrator of the film, compares teenagers' interaction at school with animal behavior in East Africa. Although she thinks like a young anthropologist, Cady cannot resist the glamour of the "Plastics," the school's leading clique. Mimicking typical high school customs, the Plastics of "Girl World" follow a strict schedule of behavior. On Wednesdays they wear pink; on Fridays they wear jeans or track pants, and once a week they put their hair in ponytails. They play phone pranks on other girls, including a call to a girl's mother to explain that her daughter's pregnancy test results are ready to pick up at Planned Parenthood and three-way calls in which one girl criticizes another without knowing that girl is listening.

All of the Plastics' nastiest thoughts about their friends go into a pink "Burn Book," which resembles traditional slam books. Toward the end of the film, when Regina (Rachel McAdams), the clique's leader, spreads pages of the Burn Book all over the school, chaos ensues. Miss Norbury (Tina Fey), a popular math teacher, tries to defuse the meanness of a large group of high school girls by making all of the girls apologize for mean things they have done. Amusingly, the girls offer backhanded apologies that cause even more hurt feelings. These apologies mirror schools' attempts to stop girls' meanness in therapeutic interventions of the early twenty-first century (Wiseman 40; Tucker 14–16).

The lighthearted "gross-out" film *How to Eat Fried Worms* (2006) begins with Billy (Luke Benward) entering his new fifth-grade classroom. Mean kids under the tutelage of class bully Joe (Adam Hicks) fill Billy's thermos with worms and give Billy a contemptuous nickname: "Worm Boy." Joe and his buddies throw candy worms at Billy, chanting his nickname until Billy claims to be a worm-eater: "The greasier, the better." After Joe dares Billy to eat 10 fried worms, the excitement begins. The boys cook worms 10 different ways, preparing a peanut-butter-and-worm sandwich, a worm fried in pig fat, and other creative dishes. Besides demonstrating the versatility of children under pressure from their peer group, *How to Eat Fried Worms* gives viewers the satisfaction of seeing the bully deposed. At the film's end, because of his eagerness to be fair, Billy joins Joe in doing what the bet requires: going to school wearing pants filled with worms.

Gangs and Clubs

Films about children's self-organized groups, sometimes called gangs, usually include a good deal of material from the childhood underground. In 1922, a series of short films titled *Our Gang* began a long, successful run. Produced by Hal Roach, this series featured a diverse group of child actors. *Our Gang's* humorous, realistic approach set a new standard for children's films. After the short film series ended in 1944, the films became part of a television series, *The Little Rascals.*

Some *Little Rascals* episodes focus on children's folklore. In "A Quiet Street" (1922), a new boy bullies little Jackie (Jackie Cooper); gang members beat up the new boy and then discover that the boy's father is a policeman. In "Lodge Night" (1923), the gang initiates a new boy into a secret club called the Cluck Cluck Klams (a parody of the name Ku Klux Klan). Other episodes show gang members starting a barbershop, a circus, a fair, and a racetrack of their own. "Shivering Spooks" (1926) portrays a séance. Several episodes demonstrate the delight of evading teachers and playing hooky. The Little Rascals Web page on TV.com (http://www.tv.com/little-rascals/show/10343/summary.html) provides detailed information on all of these early episodes.

In 1994, the feature film *The Little Rascals* introduced "Our Gang" characters to a new generation of children. The film mainly focuses on the boys' clubhouse, where no girls are allowed. Alfalfa (Bug Hall), who has fallen in love with Darla (Brittany Ashton Holmes), breaks the club's rules by inviting Darla inside for a special dinner. Besides boy/girl interaction, go-kart racing gives the film dramatic tension. The gang's go-kart, "The Blur," seems inferior to a rich boy's more expensive vehicle, but against all odds, it wins a race.

Since the late 1980s, films about skateboard gangs have reflected the popularity of skateboarding as a neighborhood pastime. In *Thrashin* (1987), members of a good skateboard gang, the Ramp Locals, feud with members of a bad gang, the Daggers. The film's climax comes when the two gangs compete in a deserted river bed; of course the "good guys" win. In contrast to this entertaining but clichéd film, *Dogtown and Z Boys* (2001) explores the history of skateboarding in Venice and Santa Monica, California. This documentary film, narrated by Sean Penn and directed by Stacy Peralta, explains how teenaged surfers helped to launch skateboarding as a sport. A feature film on the same subject, *Lords of Dogtown*, appeared in 2005.

Camp

Many films about residential camps emphasize folk traditions, which draw campers together. Camp movies run the gamut from comedy to horror. In one of the first comedies, *The Parent Trap* (1961), two girls get acquainted at Camp Inch. Identical 13-year-olds Susan and Sharon (both played by Hayley Mills) come from different parts of the United States; Susan's home is a ranch in California, while Sharon's is a palatial house with a butler in Boston. The two girls immediately dislike each other. One night Susan and some of her friends sneak into Sharon's cabin to wind string around the beds and make a mess with shaving cream and honey. After the cabin fails inspection, Sharon plans her revenge. During a dance to which boys are invited, Sharon creeps up behind Susan and cuts off the back of her dress. After this prank succeeds, the camp's director places the two girls together in a separate cabin for the last four weeks of camp. During this period of isolation, they discover that they are twin sisters, separated because of their parents' divorce.

Eager to meet the parent they have never had the chance to know, Susan and Sharon work out an elaborate plan to change places and bring their parents back together. Once they have taken on their new identities, the girls discover an obstacle: their father Mitch (Brian Keith) wants to marry an attractive young woman named Vicky (Joanna Barnes) who dislikes children. Horrified by this threat of an evil stepmother, the twins reveal their identities. Their mother (Maureen O'Hara) travels to California with Susan. During a camping trip, Susan and Sharon play a series of pranks on Vicky that culminate in her awakening to find a bear cub licking honey off her toes. Vicky calls the wedding off, leaving the twins' parents free to remarry. In the 1998 remake of *The Parent Trap*, Joanna Barnes plays the role of the girlfriend's mother. Reflecting social change, both the twins' mother and their father's girlfriend have careers of their own.

One of the earliest camp comedies, *Meatballs* (1979), features traditional pranks and legends. Camp North Star's head counselor Tripper Harrison (Bill Murray) befriends an unpopular boy, Rudy, who has no talent for sports. After Rudy wins a burping contest, he starts to feel better. Campers and counselors-in-training (CITs) pull various pranks, including lighting firecrackers and putting the camp director's bed outdoors on Parents' Day. One of the movie's high points is Tripper's narration of "The Hook," which ends with the lines "They never found the killer. Some people say he's here in the woods, waiting for the chance to kill again!" After that final line, Tripper pulls out a stainless steel hook to frighten the campers.

A later camp comedy, *Heavyweights* (1995), begins with a chaotic school scene: papers fly through the air. Gerry, the central character (Aaron Schwartz), gets upset when his parents tell him he will be spending the summer at a camp for overweight children. "It's a fat camp!" he moans, but fellow campers reassure him: "No one picks on you, because you're not the fat kid. *Everyone's* the fat kid." Folk traditions at this camp include ghost stories, go-kart races, swims out to a raft called "The Blob," and spirited subversion of the "camp food only" rule. Clever campers smuggle in salamis and other tasty snacks. Once the new camp director (Ben Stiller) arrives, a tough regimen of exercise and humiliating rituals makes the campers miserable. Against all odds, the campers defeat Camp MVP in a three-part Apache Relay. After this encouraging win, a new camp director takes charge, and life at the camp becomes pleasant again.

In contrast to camp comedies, *Friday the 13th* (1980) portrays camp as a setting for murder and mayhem. Since Jason Voorhees drowned at Camp Crystal Lake, no camper or counselor can feel safe there. This film brings to mind ghost and horror legends told by counselors to campers. In the second scene, campers peacefully sing traditional camp songs; then a "sh-sh" sound announces a killer's approach. Two counselors kiss; the boy gets stabbed, and his girlfriend screams. As in many legends, youthful sexual activity leads to death. An old man warns the current counselors, "I'm a messenger of God! You're doomed if you stay here!" After having sex, a young woman gets hit on the head with a hatchet. Besides emphasizing how dangerous sexual involvement can be for the young, *Friday the 13th* presents murders in an intriguingly ambiguous context. Is the killer Jason, who drowned in the late 1950s, or is it a living person with a grudge against young people at the camp? As in many oral ghost stories, it is difficult to discern the source of danger.

Shortly after the release of *Friday the 13th*, *The Burning* (1981) gave viewers another view of folk legends coming to life. Some critics have dismissed *The Burning* as a clone of *Friday the 13th*, but folklore and film scholar Mikel Koven recognizes it as an important part of the folkloristic social script created by slasher films (2008). Based on the "Cropsey Maniac" legend cycle documented by Lee Haring and Mark Breslerman in 1977, *The Burning* begins with a counselor's narration of the Cropsey legend at Camp Blackfoot. A flashback reveals that the counselor, Todd (Brian Matthews), participated in a prank that left the caretaker, Cropsey (Lou David), horribly burned and eager for revenge. At the end of the film, Todd kills Cropsey with the help of a camper, Alfred (Brian Backer). Koven observes that "the grown-up Alfred, now telling this tale to campers around a campfire, thereby [returns] the narrative, albeit fictively, back into the oral tradition" (126–27).

Another horror movie, *Sleepaway Camp* (1983), has become, like *Friday the 13th* and *The Burning,* a cult classic. The central character, Angela (Felissa Rose), moves in with her Aunt Martha (Desirée Gould) after losing her family in a boating accident. With her cousin Ricky (Jonathan Tiersten), shy, taciturn Angela goes to Camp Arawak for the summer. Unwilling to participate in most camp activities, she becomes the target of "mean girl" taunts from a bully named Judy (Karen Fields). Boys at the camp enjoy playing pranks; they squirt shaving cream into a sleeping bunkmate's hand, pretend that a water snake lurks near a canoe, and reminisce about hanging girls' underwear from the flagpole. Shortly after Angela and Ricky arrive at Camp Arawak, staff members and campers start to die in a series of horrible accidents. Uncertainty about the murderer's identity keeps tension high until the shocking final scene. *Sleepaway Camp II: Unhappy Campers* (1988) begins with campers listening to the story of what happened after Angela and Ricky came to Camp Arawak. In 1988 the movie's marketers issued a *Sleepaway Camp Survival Kit* containing the original movie and two of its sequels. The red ink on the cover of this survival kit feels sticky, like blood; inside the cover are pictures of band-aids, gauze, and other first aid supplies. This unusual packaging makes a point that most horror movie fans already understand: slasher classics are not just scary, but funny as well. Camp movie classics like the *Sleepaway Camp* series serve as examples of the genre of humor called *camp:* outrageous, tasteless humor that amuses the viewer because it tests boundaries of acceptability.

TELEVISION

On television, children's folklore has become part of shows of various kinds: morning shows for preschoolers, situation comedies, horror shows, and others. These shows have reflected children's interests (as well as the interests of writers and producers) and have helped to engage young viewers in folklore that used to circulate primarily through oral tradition.

In the United States, one of most widely respected morning shows for young children is *Sesame Street,* which began in 1969. Hoping to make education enjoyable for all young children, the producers of *Sesame Street* focused on inner-city children as well as children in other environments. Examination of the show's lyrics archive reveals how successfully *Sesame Street* has represented children's folklore. Traditional songs include the clapping game "Down Down Baby" and "Miss Mary M M M." The latter begins with cleverly altered wording: "Miss Mary M M M / Made mucho mess, mess, mess / Spilled chocolate milk milk milk / All down her dress dress dress" *(Sesame Street Lyrics Archive)*. Other songs, such as "Monster in the Mirror," reflect legends about mirror apparitions. Some of the most amusing songs are parodies, such as "Cereal Girl" (based on Madonna's "Material Girl") and "Chariots of Fur" (based on the theme song from the film *Chariots of Fire*).

Some television series have dramatized legends from children's and adolescents' oral tradition. Rod Serling's *Twilight Zone* (1959–64), for example, captivated young viewers with its presentation of stories that straddled the domains of folklore, fantasy literature, and science fiction. The episode "The Living Doll" (1963) introduced a doll named "Talky Tina," given as a birthday gift to a little girl named Christie. Based on children's "China Doll" legends and the popular "Chatty Cathy" doll of the 1960s, Tina uttered the memorable line "My name is Talky Tina, and I'm going to kill you." A well-developed version of the "China Doll" legend is included in chapter 3.

A more recent series, *Are You Afraid of the Dark?* (1992–96), appealed to preadolescents who were enjoying the "good scares" of slumber parties and sleepaway camp. Presented on the Nickelodeon channel for children, this series used many traditional tales and legends as a basis for its episodes. In one of the first episodes, "The Tale of the Lonely Ghost" (1992), a girl visited a haunted house, where she found a sad little ghost. "The Tale of the Phantom Cab" (1992) introduced two brothers who had gotten lost in the woods. After meeting a reclusive scientist and a mysterious cab driver, the boys saved their own lives by solving a traditional riddle. One of the most suspenseful episodes of the show's first season in 1992 was "The Tale of the Prom Queen," loosely based on the "Vanishing Hitchhiker" legend that has entertained children and adults for centuries. Jan Harold Brunvand's *The Vanishing Hitchhiker* (1981) explains this legend's travels through different cultural areas over a long period of time.

Reality television shows have also included some elements of children's folklore. *Kid Nation*, which began in the fall of 2007, showed 40 children trying to form a society of their own in the New Mexican desert. The producers divided the children into four districts—yellow, blue, green, and red—for a color war that would determine their class: upper class, merchant, cook, or laborer. At schools and summer camps, many children have played competitive games as members of color-coded teams, but *Kid Nation*'s color war gave the familiar pattern a new kind of social stratification. Besides vying for class status, the children competed for gold stars worth $20,000. One child took the role of bully, and others became the bully's targets. Fascinated and horrified by this show, journalists and others compared it to William Golding's novel *Lord of the Flies* (1954), in which children stranded on a desert island form a society of their own that disintegrates into brutal misbehavior.

Television commercials have also included children's folklore. An Oreo cookie commercial in the summer of 2007, for example, shows boys at camp passing along a message by whispering in each others' ears. The first boy whispers "Billy's got an Oreo cakester!" When the chain of transmission ends, the message has become "Billy's got his first chest hair!" This commercial succeeds in getting viewers' attention by combining a familiar summer camp scene with a popular message-whispering game that is often called Telephone. This commercial reminds viewers of the importance of "firsts" in the march toward maturity.

TOYS AND GAMES

While mass-produced toys differ from folk toys made by children, they intersect with children's folklore in many ways. In *Toys As Culture* (1986), Brian Sutton-Smith analyzes toys' functions in children's daily lives. Toys express bonds and obligations between parents and children; they amuse and console children who are playing alone. In addition, toys become part of children's identities and education. Sutton-Smith explains that toys "are in *marked contrast* with the everyday world which they represent, or to which they refer, or in which they have their existence" (249). Children may follow cultural rules when they play with toys; alternatively, they may defy or subvert those rules.

Sometimes children make their own rules to supplement or replace the rules of commercial games. Players of the board game Monopoly, for example, can decide to place money paid in fines under the "Free Parking" space. The lucky person who lands on that space collects all the money that has accumulated there. Some groups of players allow certain kinds of cheating, but others frown on such expansion of the rules of the game.

Another game, the Parker Brothers' Ouija board, became available in stores in 1966. Both before and after this game's commercial release, children have followed rules learned from each other; they tend to take Ouija boards very seriously. Variants of Ouija board usage have existed since the time of Pythagoras in ancient Greece. Contemporary American children tell each other to use the Ouija board carefully; they warn each other against using Ouija boards alone and suggest that throwing a Ouija board away may result in dangerous consequences. Films such as *Witchboard* (1986) dramatize young people's fears about results of improper Ouija board use.

An important source of traditional knowledge for children has been the series of "how-to" kits introduced by Klutz Inc. in the 1980s. All of these kits include a book and a toy or craft materials. Klutz kits bring to mind the marketing strategy of John Newbery's *Little Pretty Pocket-Book,* sold with a ball and pincushion in 1744. The Klutz *Book of Jacks* (1988) includes a small bag of jacks, and the *Cootie Catcher Book* (1998) comes with material for making paper fortune-tellers. Other books in the series show children how to play Chinese jump rope and to make paper airplanes and other toys.

Some commercially marketed card games have important folk elements. In the game of Spoons, for example, children rapidly pass cards around a circle; the first player who gets a complete set of cards of one suit grabs a spoon, and all the other players reach for spoons as quickly as possible. While it is possible to play Spoons with an old deck of cards and a handful of ordinary spoons, the commercial Spoons game offers a new deck of cards, a pile of plastic spoons, and a list of rules. Another card game, Dutch Blitz, has been popular among Mennonite young people. This game involves a special deck of cards featuring pictures of farm implements and other objects. According to Andrew Lewis, some Mennonite families modify the game's rules to suit their own preferences; others bake cupcakes decorated with frosting designs that match the cards ("Dutch Blitz").

In contrast to card games, video games have alarmed parents and educators. Brian Sutton-Smith suggests that the video game, "a vehicle of solitary concentration," "not only isolates the child; it possesses the child" (*Toys* 75). Fear of their children becoming obsessed by video games has made some parents impose playtime restrictions. Not all children play video games alone; some interact with siblings and friends while playing. Video game tournaments organized by children offer exciting competition.

Some best-selling video games use patterns related to heroic quests in the traditional folktale. Nintendo's "Super Mario Brothers" (1985), for example, sends the hero on a race through a mushroom kingdom to defeat enemies and rescue a princess. In the Nintendo 64 game "The Legend of Zelda: The Ocarina of Time" (1998), the lead character, Link, finds Princess Zelda in Hyrule Castle. Princess Zelda tells Link that he must find three sacred stones and take possession of the power-filled Triforce before the desert king Ganondorf gets it. In games like this one, the child player becomes a hero, fighting with evildoers and completing a complex quest.

DOLLS

Children have played with dolls made of wood, stone, clay, paper, bone, and other materials since prehistoric times. Dolls made by women at home have included Haudenosaunee (Iroquois) "no face" cornhusk dolls and Appalachian applehead dolls. In many cultures, dolls are associated with good luck and prosperity.

According to Elizabeth Cameron and Doran Ross, Ashanti dolls in West Africa, for example, serve as playthings and promoters of fertility. Japanese *daruma* dolls have no eyes when purchased; after the new doll's owner makes a wish and finds that the wish comes true, it is time for the owner to give the doll an eye or eyes. Doll play has been well documented in Japan; the novel *The Tale of Genji*, attributed to Lady Murasaki in the early eleventh century, describes girls' play with dolls and dollhouses. Each year in March, Japanese girls celebrate the traditional Doll Festival, also known as Girls' Day.

Europe became a center of doll manufacturing in the fifteenth century, with Germany and France taking the lead. At the beginning of the twentieth century, Josephine Scribner Gates's "live doll" stories encouraged little girls to treat their dolls as if they were live human beings; her books became popular among American girls. After World War I, American doll manufacturing increased; the invention of plastics made dolls cheaper and more widely available in the second half of the twentieth century. Most contemporary accounts of children's doll play describe creative play with relatively inexpensive plastic dolls.

Barbie dolls, first marketed in 1959, have become icons of American culture. Mary F. Rogers, author of *Barbie Culture* (1999), states that Barbie has "a mutable, protean, impression-managing, context-bound self whose demeanor shifts from situation to situation and from role to role" (137). Since Barbie has innumerable outfits and accessories, she encourages children's acquisition of more and more things. The antidote to this galloping consumerism is "folk Barbie," explicated in Jeannie B. Thomas's wonderful book *Naked Barbies, Warrior Joes, and Other Forms of Visible Gender*. Thomas observes that Barbie takes many roles during children's doll play: "She shops, goes to college, makes sushi, has sex with aliens, gets pregnant, and works at jobs ranging from babysitter to dentist to stewardess to architect. She participates in race-car driving, camping, dating, swimming, mountain climbing, and movie watching" (134). Some children have removed their Barbie dolls' heads and baked the heads in ovens or flushed them down the toilet (114).

Like Barbie, G. I. Joe action figures have inspired creative play. It is important to note that gender stereotyping had a role in the marketing of G. I. Joe figures, which came out in 1964. Intended primarily for boys, these plastic figures emphasized "action" rather than the hairstyles and special outfits that characterized Barbie. Jeannie B. Thomas notes that G. I. Joe's large biceps reflect American society's admiration for masculine power (119). Thomas's interviews with children who have played with Barbie and G. I. Joe reveal that folk games give both dolls a broader range of roles than their creators had in mind. Sometimes G. I. Joe takes the role of Barbie's son; other times he serves as a critic for fashion shows starring Barbie and her consort Ken (134–35).

Mass-produced American Halloween costumes have given kids the opportunity to dress up as Barbie, G. I. Joe, Supergirl, Superman, Harry Potter, Wonder

California baby boy dressed as Benjamin Bunny for Halloween, 2006. Photograph by Buzz Hays.

Woman, Teenage Mutant Ninja Turtles, and other well-known figures. It is not unusual for babies and dogs to wear Halloween costumes of their own. Children begin participating in Halloween by wearing costumes their parents have bought or made, but as they get older, they may choose to make costumes that reflect their own imaginations.

Some dolls have associated themselves with horror legends in interesting ways. Hasbro's "My Buddy" doll, released in 1985, resembles the "Chucky" doll that becomes a demonic killer in the horror movie *Child's Play* (1988). These movies have become cult classics, with the hilarious *Bride of Chucky* (1998) generating a line of bride dolls that has delighted both children and adults.

More peaceful and aesthetically appealing dolls have come from the American Girl doll company, founded by educator Pleasant Rowland in 1985. This company offers historically accurate facsimiles of American children's clothes, pets, and playthings from the colonial era to the present. Each doll, which comes with a set of books about her adventures, is described as the "star of her story." Orphaned Samantha, who represents the Victorian era, has a three-wheeled bicycle, a tea-tin lunchbox, a doll pram, and ice skates. Addy, enslaved on a plantation in the 1860s, has a tin pail lunchbox and ice cream party treats. Josefina, whose family owns a ranch in New Mexico in the 1820s, has a weaving loom, riding boots, an adobe oven, and a niña doll, as well as Christmas accessories that reflect Hispanic holiday traditions: two strings of red chili peppers and a wooden lantern for *La Posada* processions. And Kaya, a Nez Perce girl growing up in 1764, has a horse with a special saddle, a porcupine-quill necklace, a baby doll with cradleboard, and huckleberries and camas roots inside a leather pouch. Through these heirloom dolls, children learn about folkways of children from diverse ethnicities and historical periods.

Some twenty-first-century dolls have generated controversy. Bratz Dolls, first manufactured in 2001, have wide eyes, tiny noses, and feet attached to high-fashion shoes; much of their clothing looks alluring. Wildly popular in Spain, France, Israel, Italy, the United Kingdom, and the United States, these dolls have alarmed parents, teachers, and scholars of childhood. In 2007 the American Psychological Association's "Task Force on Sexualization of Girls" commented that Bratz dolls, which wear fishnet stockings, miniskirts, and feather boas, sexually objectify young women.

In play therapy, dolls help children express their needs. Virginia M. Axline's *Dibs in Search of Self* (1986) explains how a little boy overcomes adjustment difficulties through regular doll play in his therapist's office. *Play and Intervention* (1994), edited by Joop Hellendoorn, Rimmert van der Kooij, and Brian Sutton-Smith, covers a wide range of therapies involving dolls and toys. One of this book's essays, Jerome L. Singer's "Scientific Foundation of Play Therapy," explains that the "cognitive revolution of twentieth-century psychology resulted in a wide range of interventions" (27). Psychologists have developed academic play programs and play therapies for children with autism and other special needs.

In his 2008 essay "To Play or Not to Play," Sutton-Smith states, "In the 21st century virtually any activity is considered superior to doing nothing." Noting educators' preference for all that seems "useful," Sutton-Smith argues that "play has its *own* purposes that are more fundamental." Studying these purposes will provide interesting and important work for future folklorists of childhood.

WORKS CITED

Alcott, Louisa May. *Little Women*. 1867. New York: Penguin, 1989.

Au Revoir, Les Enfants. VHS. Directed by Louis Malle. 1987. New York: Orion Home Video, 1990.

Axline, Virginia. *Dibs in Search of Self*. New York: Ballantine, 1986.

Bader, Barbara, and Arthur Geisert. *Aesop and Company with Scenes from his Legendary Life*. New York: Houghton, 1992.

The Belles of St. Trinian's. DVD. Directed by Frank Launder. 1954. Baker City, OR: Hollywood's Attic, 2006.

Blume, Judy. *Are You There, God? It's Me, Margaret.* 1970. New York: Random House, 1991.

———. *Blubber.* 1974. New York: Random House, 1986.

———. *Forever.* 1975. New York: Simon and Schuster, 2007.

———. *Then Again, Maybe I Won't.* 1971. New York: Random House, 1986.

Brink, Carol Ryrie. *Caddie Woodlawn.* 1935. New York: Aladdin, 1990.

Brunvand, Jan H. *The Vanishing Hitchhiker.* New York: Norton, 1981.

Burnett, Frances Hodgson. *The Secret Garden.* 1909. New York: Harper Trophy, 1998.

The Burning. DVD. Directed by Tony Maylam. 1981. Beverly Hills, CA: Twentieth Century Fox Home Entertainment, 2007.

Cameron, Elizabeth Lynn, and Doran H. Ross. *Isn't S/He a Doll: Play and Ritual in African Sculpture.* Los Angeles: UCLA Fowler Museum of Cultural History, 1996.

Carroll, Lewis. *Alice's Adventures in Wonderland.* 1865. New York: Random House, 1946.

———. *Through the Looking Glass.* 1871. Boston: Adamant, 2001.

Cleary, Beverly. *Beezus and Ramona.* 1955. New York: Harper Trophy, 1990.

———. *Henry and the Clubhouse.* 1962. New York: Harper Trophy, 1990.

———. *Henry Huggins.* 1950. New York: Harper Trophy, 1990.

———. *Ramona Forever.* 1984. New York: Avon Camelot, 1995.

Clinton, Hillary Rodham. "An Idyllic Childhood." *The Games We Played.* Ed. Steven A. Cohen. New York: Simon and Schuster, 2001. 161–65.

———. *Living History.* New York: Simon and Schuster, 2003.

The Craft. DVD. Directed by Andrew Fleming. 1996. Culver City, CA: Sony Pictures, 1997.

Dogtown and Z Boys. DVD. Directed by Stacy Peralta. 2001. Culver City, CA: SONY Pictures, 2002.

Ferris Bueller's Day Off. DVD. Directed by John Hughes. 1986. Hollywood, CA: Paramount, 1999.

Friday the 13th. DVD. 1980. Directed by Sean S. Cunningham. Hollywood, CA: Paramount, 1999.

Gates, Josephine Scribner. *The Story of Live Dolls.* Indianapolis: Bowen-Merrill, 1901.

Gilbreth, Frank B. *Cheaper by the Dozen.* New York: Crowell, 1948.

Golding, William. 1954. *Lord of the Flies.* New York: Coward-McCann, 1962.

Haring, Lee, and Mark Breslerman. "The Cropsey Maniac." *New York Folklore* 3.1–4 (1977): 15–27.

Hearn, Julie. *The Minister's Daughter.* New York and London: Atheneum, 2005.

Heavyweights. DVD. Directed by Steven Brill. 1995. Burbank, CA: Walt Disney Video, 2003.

Hellendoorn, Joop, Rimmert van der Kooij, and Brian Sutton-Smith, eds. *Play and Intervention.* Albany: SUNY Press, 1994.

Howard, Dorothy Mills. *Dorothy's World: Childhood in Sabine Bottom, 1902–1910.* Englewood Cliffs, NJ: Prentice-Hall, 1977.

How to Eat Fried Worms. DVD. Directed by Bob Dolman. New York: New Line Home Video, 2006.

Hurston, Zora Neale. *Dust Tracks on a Road.* Urbana: U of Illinois P, 1984.

Kimmel, Eric A., and Erika Weihs. *Days of Awe: Stories for Rosh Hashanah and Yom Kippur.* New York: Viking, 1992.

Kirshenblatt, Mayer, and Barbara Kirshenblatt-Gimblett. *They Called Me Mayer July: Painted Memories of a Jewish Childhood in Poland before the Holocaust.* Berkeley: U of California P, 2007.

Klutz, Inc. *Book of Jacks.* Palo Alto, CA: Klutz, 1988.

Klutz, Inc. *Cootie Catcher Book.* Palo Alto, CA: Klutz, 1998.

Koven, Mikel J. *Film, Folklore, and Urban Legends.* Lanham, MD: Scarecrow Press, 2008.

Kübler-Ross, Elisabeth. *The Wheel of Life: A Memoir of Living and Dying.* New York: Simon and Schuster, 1997.

Lewis, Andrew David. "Dutch Blitz Tradition." Unpublished essay, Wayne State University, 2006.

Lewis, C. S. *The Silver Chair.* 1953. New York: Collier, 1971.

———. *Surprised by Joy.* London: Bles, 1955.

"Little Rascals." TV.com. 2008. http://www.tv.com/little-rascals/show/10343/summary.html.

The Little Rascals. VHS. Directed by Penelope Spheeris. 1994. Universal City, CA: Universal Studios, 1995.

"The Living Doll." *The Twilight Zone,* originally aired November 1, 1963, CBS.

Lords of Dogtown. DVD. Directed by Catherine Hardwicke. Culver City, CA: Sony Pictures, 2005.

McManus, Blanche. *Our Little Scotch Cousin.* Boston: Page, 1906.

Mean Girls. DVD. Directed by Mark Waters. Hollywood, CA: Paramount, 2004.

Meatballs. DVD. Directed by Ivan Reitman. 1979. New York: HBO Home Video, 1999.

Mergen, Bernard. *Play and Playthings.* Westport: Greenwood, 1982.

Murasaki, Lady. *The Tale of Genji,* tr. Arthur Waley. Boston: Houghton-Mifflin, 1925.

Newbery, John. *A Little Pretty Pocket-Book, Intended for the Instruction and Amusement of Little Master Tommy and Pretty Miss Polly.* 1744. Worcester, MA: Isaiah Thomas, 1787.

The Parent Trap. DVD. Directed by Nancy Meyers. 1998. Burbank, CA: Walt Disney Video, 2004.

The Parent Trap. VHS. Directed by David Swift. 1961. Burbank, CA: Walt Disney Video, 1995.

Les Quatre Cents Coups [The 400 Blows]. DVD. Directed by François Truffaut. 1959. New York: Criterion, 2006.

Rodden, John. *Conversations with Isabel Allende.* Austin: U of Texas P, 2004.

Rogers, Mary F. *Barbie Culture.* London: Sage, 1999.

Rowling, J. K. *Harry Potter and the Sorcerer's Stone.* New York: Scholastic, 1997.

Sesame Street Lyrics Archive. 2007. http://members.tripod.com/Tiny-dancer/sesame1.html.

Singer, Jerome L. "The Scientific Foundations of Play Therapy." *Play and Intervention.* Ed. Joop Hellendoorn, Rimmert van der Kooij, and Brian Sutton-Smith. Albany: State U of New York P, 1994. 27–38.

Sleepaway Camp. DVD. Directed by Robert Hiltzik. 1983. Troy, MI: Anchor Bay Entertainment, 2000.

Sleepaway Camp II: Unhappy Campers. DVD. Directed by Michael A. Simpson. 1988. Troy, MI: Anchor Bay Entertainment, 2002.

Sutton-Smith, Brian. "A Play Biography." *Children's Folklore Review* 20.1–2 (1997–98): 5–42.

———. "To Play or Not to Play: Grownups, Kids and the War on Recess." *Pennsylvania Gazette.* Jan.–Feb. 2008. http://www.upenn.edu/Gazette/0108/expert.html.

———. *Toys As Culture.* New York: Gardner, 1986.

"The Tale of the Lonely Ghost." *Are You Afraid of the Dark?,* originally aired August 29, 1992, Nickelodeon.

"The Tale of the Phantom Cab." *Are You Afraid of the Dark?,* originally aired July 16, 1992, Nickelodeon.

"The Tale of the Prom Queen." *Are You Afraid of the Dark?,* originally aired November 7, 1992, Nickelodeon.

Thomas, Jeannie Banks. *Naked Barbies, Warrior Joes, and Other Forms of Visible Gender.* Urbana: U of Illinois P, 2003.

Thrashin. DVD. Directed by David Winters. 1987. Los Angeles, CA: MGM, 2003.

Thwe, Pascal Khoo. *From the Land of Green Ghosts: A Burmese Odyssey.* New York: Harper-Perennial, 2003.

Tolkien, J.R.R. *The Hobbit: 70th Anniversary Edition.* 1938. New York: Houghton, 2007.

The Trouble With Angels. DVD. Directed by Ida Lupino. 1966. Culver City, CA: Sony Pictures, 2003.

Tucker, Elizabeth. "'Mean Girls': The Reclassification of Children's and Adolescents' Folklore." *Children's Folklore Review* 25.1–2 (2002–03): 7–22.

Twain, Mark. *The Adventures of Tom Sawyer.* 1871. New York: Sterling, 2004. Wade, Mary Hazleton. *Our Little Indian Cousin.* Boston: Page, 1901.

Walls, Jeannette. *The Glass Castle.* New York: Simon and Schuster, 2006.

Wilder, Laura Ingalls. *Little House in the Big Woods.* 1932. New York: Harper and Row, 1971.

———. *Little House on the Prairie.* 1935. New York: Harper and Row, 1971.

Wiseman, Rosalind. *Queen Bees and Wannabes: Helping Your Daughter Survive Cliques, Gossip, Boyfriends, and Other Realities of Adolescence.* New York: Crown, 2002.

Witchboard. DVD. Directed by Kevin S. Tenney. 1986. Troy, MI: Anchor Bay Entertainment, 2004.

Zéro de Conduite [Zero for Conduct]. VHS. Directed by Jean Vigo. 1933. Chatsworth, CA: Home Vision Entertainment, 2001.

Glossary

Catch. An embarrassing riddle conclusion; alternatively, a folktale ending that involves a surprise or grab.

Childhood underground. As defined by Mary and Herbert Knapp (1976), the childhood underground is the transmission system by which children learn from each other, with minimal or no adult interference.

Childlore. Children's folklore.

Contemporary legend. A term that became common in the early 1990s. Contemporary legends express current interests and concerns.

Context. Information related to the collection of a legend text or another kind of folklore: location, circumstances, mood, presence of other people, and any other relevant factors.

Dialectics. As defined by Linda Dégh and Andrew Vázsonyi (1976), a legend-telling process that involves belief, partial belief, and skepticism, all of which make the legend a lively genre.

Divination. Guessing or foretelling the future, as in predicting who one's future spouse will be while jumping rope.

Double Dutch. A jump-rope style involving two ropes or one doubled rope, turned very quickly.

Dozens. Humorous insults from the African American tradition.

Fieldworker. Someone who collects folklore.

Folk. People who share various forms of traditional learning.

Folklore. Traditional learning shared by people in small or larger groups.

Fort. An indoor or outdoor shelter built by children.

Freudian. Characteristic of the theory of Sigmund Freud (1856–1939), the Austrian neurologist who founded psychoanalysis.

Function. The purpose served by folklore.

Funny-scary story. A tale that begins in a frightening way but ends humorously.

Genre. A particular kind of folklore: for example, the legend, the folktale, or the joke.

Ghost story. A story about supernatural characters or events.

Halloween. The evening of October 31, when, according to British and American folk tradition, ghosts walk and tricks take place; some communities have a separate "Mischief Night."

Informant. Someone who shares an item of folklore with a fieldworker.

Initiation. The process by which someone becomes part of a group.

Legend. A genre of folk narrative, usually "told as true," featuring real-seeming characters and events.

Ludic. Playful.

Memorate. A first-person narrative based on individual experience.

Motif. A small unit of folklore that can be studied cross-culturally.

Motif index. Stith Thompson's *Motif-Index of Folk-Literature,* first published from 1955 to 1958.

Narrative. Prose that tells about sequential events; synonym for *story.*

Narrator. Teller of a story.

Newell's paradox. As defined by Gary Alan Fine (1980), William Wells Newell's assertion that children are both highly conservative and extremely creative.

Oral tradition. Tradition transmitted primarily by word of mouth.

Ostension. As defined by Linda Dégh and Andrew Vázsonyi, enactment of a legend or part of a legend in a serious, sometimes harmful way.

Parody. A humorous imitation of a song, story, or other expressive form.

Prank. An outrageous practical joke.

Psychoanalytic analysis. Analysis of folklore narratives in relation to the theories of Sigmund Freud, Carl Jung, and Joseph Campbell, with particular attention to sexual symbolism.

Riddlee. A person who tries to come up with the answer to a riddle.

Riddler. A person who tells a riddle.

Ritual. A repeated pattern of behavior.

Routine of victimization. A relatively short interaction during which one child embarrasses another or causes brief pain or discomfort.

Rumor. An unconfirmed statement, closely related to the legend.

Screenname. A name chosen for use online; in many cases, this name differs from the individual's actual name.

Subversion. An attempt to undermine the authority of dominant individuals, such as parents or teachers, or of the dominant culture.

Tale. A short narrative with a fictional plot.

Taunt. A malicious verbal assault, sometimes called a jeer.

Taw. An object thrown on the ground to play Hopscotch.

Tease. A playful form of verbal criticism.

Tradition. Material that is passed along from one person to another and from one generation to the next.

Transmission. The process of sharing folklore, either orally or by example.

Triviality barrier. As defined by Gary Alan Fine, adults' failure to pay attention to children's folklore because they perceive it as trivial.

Type. A pattern of episodes that stays together in a folktale.

Type index. Antti Aarne's and Stith Thompson's *The Types of the Folktale,* first published in 1928.

Urban legend. Often but not always found in urban areas, the urban legend recounts sensational, shocking, and amazing events; this term entered common usage in the early 1980s.

Variant. A text that represents a certain kind of folk narrative (or of another genre of folklore).

Version. Generally synonymous with *variant.*

YouTube. Internet technology that makes it possible for individuals to share their own videos with a large audience online.

Bibliography

REFERENCE WORKS

Aarne, Antti, and Stith Thompson. *The Types of the Folktale: A Classification and Bibliography.* 1928. Helsinki: Suomalainen Tiedeakatemia, 1961. The original type index, Antti Aarne's *Verzeichnis der Märchentypen*, was published in 1910.

Brown, Mary Ellen, and Bruce Rosenberg, eds. *Encyclopedia of Folklore and Literature.* Santa Barbara: ABC-CLIO, 1998.

Brunvand, Jan H. *American Folklore: An Encyclopedia.* New York: Garland, 1996.

———. *Encyclopedia of Urban Legends.* Santa Barbara: ABC-CLIO, 2001.

Christiansen, Reidar T. *The Migratory Legends.* Folklore Fellows Communications 175. Helsinki: Suomalainen Tiedeakatemia, 1958.

Leach, Maria, ed., and Jerome Fried, assoc. ed. *Funk and Wagnalls Standard Dictionary of Folklore, Mythology, and Legend.* San Francisco: Harper, 1984.

MacDonald, Margaret Read. *The Storyteller's Sourcebook: A Subject, Title, and Motif Index to Folklore Collections for Children.* Detroit: Neal-Schuman, 1982.

MacDonald, Margaret Read, Barre Toelken, Linda Dégh, and John Holmes McDowell, eds. *Traditional Storytelling Today: An International Sourcebook.* London: Taylor and Francis, 1998.

Opie, Iona, and Peter Opie. *The Oxford Dictionary of Nursery Rhymes.* 1951. Oxford: Clarendon, 1973.

Thompson, Stith. *Motif-Index of Folk Literature: A Classification of Narrative Elements in Folktales, Ballads, Myths, Fables, Mediaeval Romances, Exempla, Fabliaux, Jest-Books, and Local Legends.* Rev. and enl. ed. 6 vols. Bloomington: Indiana UP, 2000.

CHILDREN'S FOLKLORE STUDIES

Avedon, Elliott M., and Brian Sutton-Smith. *The Study of Games.* New York: Wiley, 1971.

Beckwith, Martha Warren. *Jamaica Folk-Lore.* 1928. New York: Kraus, 1969.

Bishop, Julia C., and Mavis Curtis. *Play Today in the Primary School Playground.* Buckingham, Eng., and Philadelphia: Open UP, 2001.

Brady, Margaret K. *"Some Kind of Power": Navajo Children's Skinwalker Narratives.* Salt Lake City: U of Utah P, 1984.

Bronner, Simon J. *American Children's Folklore.* Little Rock: August, 1988.

Brunvand, Jan Harold. *The Baby Train.* New York: Norton, 1993.

———. *The Choking Doberman.* New York: Norton, 1984.

———. *The Vanishing Hitchhiker.* New York: Norton, 1981.

Calvert, Karin. *Children in the House: The Material Culture of Childhood, 1600–1900.* Boston: Northeastern UP, 1992.

Carpenter, Carole Henderson. *In Our Own Image: The Child, Canadian Culture, and Our Future.* Toronto: Robarts Centre for Canadian Studies, 1996.

Chesanow, Jeanne R. *Honeysuckle Sipping: The Plant Lore of Childhood.* Camden, ME: Down East, 1987.

Chudacoff, Howard P. *Children at Play: An American History.* New York: New York UP, 2007.

Cooper, Martha. *Street Play.* New York: From Here to Fame, 2006.

Dargan, Amanda, and Steven Zeitlin. *City Play.* New Brunswick, NJ: Rutgers UP, 1990.

Darian-Smith, Kate, and June Factor. *Child's Play: Dorothy Howard and the Folklore of Australian Children.* Melbourne: Museum Victoria, 2005.

Dégh, Linda. *Legend and Belief.* Bloomington: Indiana UP, 2001.

Douglas, Norman. *London Street Games.* 1916. London: Chatto and Windus, 1931.

Dundes, Alan. *Bloody Mary in the Mirror: Essays in Psychoanalytic Folkloristics.* Jackson: UP of Mississippi, 2002.

Earle, Alice Morse. *Child Life in Colonial Days.* New York: Macmillan, 1898.

Ellis, Bill. *Aliens, Ghosts, and Cults: Legends We Live.* Jackson: UP of Mississippi, 2003.

———. *Lucifer Ascending: The Occult in Folklore and Popular Culture.* Lexington: UP of Kentucky, 2004.

———. *Raising the Devil.* Jackson: UP of Mississippi, 2000.

Factor, June. *Captain Cook Chased a Chook: Children's Folklore in Australia.* [New York]: Penguin, 1988.

———. *Kidspeak: A Dictionary of Australian Children's Words, Expressions and Games.* Melbourne: U of Melbourne, 2000.

Fowke, Edith. *Sally Go Round the Sun: 300 Songs, Rhymes and Games of Canadian Children.* Toronto: McClelland and Stewart, 1969.

Gaignebet, Claude. *Le Folklore Obscène des Enfants* [Obscene Folklore of Children]. Paris: G.-P. Maisonneuve et Larose, 1974.

Gaunt, Kyra D. *The Games Black Girls Play: Learning the Ropes from Double-Dutch to Hip-Hop.* New York: New York UP, 2006.

Goldstein, Diane E., Sylvia Ann Grider, and Jeannie Banks Thomas. *Haunting Experiences: Ghosts in Contemporary Folklore.* Logan: Utah State UP, 2007.

Gomme, Alice B. *The Traditional Games of England, Scotland, and Ireland.* 2 vols. 1894–98. New York: Dover, 1964.

———. *Old English Singing Games.* London: David Nutt.

Gomme, Alice B., and Cecil J. Sharp, eds. *Children's Singing Games*. 1909–12. New York: Arno, 1976.

Gomme, Laurence, and Alice B. Gomme. *British Folklore, Folk-Songs, and Singing Games*. London: David Nutt, 1916.

Goodwin, Marjorie Harness. *He-Said-She-Said: Talk As Social Organization among Black Children*. Bloomington: Indiana UP, 1991.

———. *The Hidden Life of Girls: Games of Stance, Status, and Exclusion*. Boston: Blackwell, 2006.

Green, Joanne, and J.D.A. Widdowson. *Traditional English Language Genres: Continuity and Change, 1950–2000*. Sheffield: National Centre for English Cultural Tradition, 2003.

Grider, Sylvia Ann. "The Supernatural Narratives of Children." Diss., Indiana U, 1976.

Hastings, Scott E., Jr. *Miss Mary Mac All Dressed in Black: Children's Lore from New England*. Little Rock: August, 1990.

Jones, Bessie, and Bess Lomax Hawes. *Step It Down: Games, Plays, Songs, and Stories from the Afro-American Heritage*. New York: Harper and Row, 1972.

Kalliala, Marjatta. *Play Culture in a Changing World*. Maidenhead, Eng.: Open UP, 2006.

Kirshenblatt-Gimblett, Barbara. *Speech Play: Research and Resources for Studying Linguistic Creativity*. Philadelphia: U of Pennsylvania P, 1976.

Knapp, Mary, and Herbert Knapp. *One Potato, Two Potato: The Secret Education of American Children*. New York: Norton, 1976.

McDowell, John Holmes. *Children's Riddling*. Bloomington: Indiana UP, 1979.

———. "The Speech Play and Verbal Art of Chicano Children: An Ethnographic and Sociolinguistic Survey." Diss., U of Texas at Austin, 1975.

McMahon, Felicia R. *Not Just Child's Play: Emerging Tradition and the Lost Boys of Sudan*. Jackson: UP of Mississippi, 2007.

Mechling, Jay. *On My Honor: Boy Scouts and the Making of American Youth*. Chicago: U of Chicago P, 2001.

Mergen, Bernard. *Play and Playthings*. Westport: Greenwood, 1982.

Opie, Iona. *The People in the Playground*. New York: Oxford UP, 1993.

Opie, Iona, and Peter Opie. *Children's Games in Street and Playground*. New York: Oxford UP, 1969.

———. *I Saw Esau: Traditional Rhymes of Youth*. London: Williams and Norgate, 1947.

———. *The Lore and Language of Schoolchildren*. New York: Oxford UP, 1959.

———. *The Singing Game*. New York: Oxford UP, 1985.

Roemer, Danielle. "A Social Interactional Analysis of Anglo Children's Folklore: Catches and Narratives." Diss., U of Texas at Austin, 1977.

Russell, Heather. *Play and Friendships in a Multi-Cultural Playground*. Melbourne: Australian Children's Folklore Publications, 1986.

Santino, Jack. *Halloween and Other Festivals of Death and Life*. Knoxville: U of Tennessee P, 1994.

Sherman, Josepha, and T.K.F. Weisskopf. *Greasy Grimy Gopher Guts: The Subversive Folklore of Childhood*. Little Rock: August, 1995.

Shuman, Amy. *Storytelling Rights: The Uses of Oral and Written Texts by Urban Adolescents.* Cambridge: Cambridge UP, 1986.

Smith, Paul, ed. *Perspectives on Contemporary Legend.* Sheffield: Centre for English Cultural Tradition and Language, 1984.

Strutt, Joseph. *Sports and Pastimes of the People of England.* London: Tegg, 1801.

Sutton-Smith, Brian. *The Ambiguity of Play.* Cambridge: Harvard UP, 1998.

———. *The Folkgames of Children.* Austin: U of Texas P, 1972.

———. *The Folkstories of Children.* Philadelphia: U of Pennsylvania P, 1981.

———. *The Games of New Zealand Children.* Los Angeles and Berkeley: U of California P, 1959.

———. *A History of Children's Play: The New Zealand Playground 1840–1950.* Philadelphia: U of Pennsylvania P, 1981.

Sutton-Smith, Brian, Jay Mechling, Thomas W. Johnson, and Felicia R. McMahon, eds. *Children's Folklore: A Source Book.* New York: Garland, 1995.

Tucker, Elizabeth. "Tradition and Creativity in the Storytelling of Pre-Adolescent Girls." Diss., Indiana U, 1977.

Turner, Ian. *Cinderella Dressed in Yella.* Melbourne: Heinemann, 1969.

Virtanen, Leea. *Children's Lore.* Studia Fennica 22. Helsinki: Suomalisen Kirjallisuuden Seura, 1978.

Whatley, Mariamne H., and Elissa R. Henken. *Did You Hear about the Girl Who…?: Contemporary Legends, Folklore, and Human Sexuality.* New York: New York UP, 2000.

Widdowson, John D. A. *If You Don't Be Good: Verbal Social Control in Newfoundland.* Social and Economic Studies 21. St. John's, Newfoundland: Institute of Social and Economic Research, 1977.

Wolfenstein, Martha. *Children's Humor: A Psychological Analysis.* New York: Free, 1954. Bloomington: Indiana UP, 1978.

Zeitlin, Steven J., Amy J. Kotkin, and Holly Cutting Baker. *A Celebration of American Family Folklore.* Cambridge, MA: Yellow Moon, 1982.

Web Resources

INTRODUCTION

The World Wide Web offers children's folklore researchers an exciting range of source material. Before the 1990s, people who wanted to learn about children's folklore had to take books out of libraries and gather material from archives. Although library and archival sources still offer excellent source material, Web sites provide some of the most up-to-date examples. Some Web sites encourage submissions of children's folklore texts by visitors, so the range of available data is always changing.

Although the Internet facilitates rapid research, it is important to remember that not all Web sites are equally trustworthy. Sites with the suffix ".com" belong to businesses; sites with the suffix ".org" belong to organizations, and sites with the suffix ".edu" belong to educational institutions. Most ".edu" sites provide reliable information; many organizational and commercial sites also offer fine material. Nonetheless, it is important to consider each Web site's validity.

Because Web sites come and go, one cannot be sure that all the sites on a list of resources will continue to be available. To maximize availability, I have listed well-established Web sites. If any of these sites seem difficult to find, I recommend trying a keyword search.

This section is designed to help researchers find accurate children's folklore texts and contextual information. Some of the best material comes from folklore archives; certain archives can be accessed online, but others require phone calls or visits. As more archives develop digital resources, it will become easier to do children's folklore research online.

SEARCH ENGINES

Reliable search engines greatly increase the efficiency of Web research. One of the best search engines is Google (http://www.google.com). Google Scholar (http://www.scholargoogle.com) offers an extensive database of full-text articles. Other effective search engines include:

All the Web (http://www.alltheweb.com)

Alta Vista (http://www.altavista.com)

DMOZ (http://www.dmoz.org)

Excite (http://www.excite.com)

Webcrawler (http://www.webcrawler.com)

Yahoo! (http://www.yahoo.com)

FOLKLORE ARCHIVES

Archive of Folk Culture, American Folklife Center, Library of Congress, Washington, D.C. (http://www.loc.gov/folklife/archive.html)

Australian Children's Folklore Collection, Museum Victoria (http://museumvictoria. com.au/DiscoveryCentre/Infosheets/ Australian_Childrens_Folklore_Collection/)

Fife Folklore Archives, Utah State University (http://library.usu.edu/Folklo/)

Folklore and Mythology Archives, University of California at Los Angeles (http:// www.humnet.ucla.edu/humnet/folklore/archives)

Folklore Archive, University of California at Berkeley (http://ls.berkeley.edu/dept/ folklore/archive-policy.html)

Folklore Archive, Wayne State University Archives (http://www.reuther.wayne.edu/ collections/collections.html)

Niagara Frontier Folklore Archives (http://buffalolore.buffalonet.org/archives/Folklore Archives.htm)

Northeast Archives of Folklore and Oral History, Maine Folklife Center, University of Maine at Orono (http://www.umaine.edu/folklife/index.htm)

Northern Virginia Folklife Archive, George Mason University (http://www.gmu.edu/ folklore/nvfa)

Public Sector Folklore Listserv Archives (http://lists.nau.edu/archives.publore.html)

University of Pennsylvania Folklore and Ethnography Archive (http://www.sas.upenn. edu/folklore/center/archive.html)

Western Kentucky University Manuscripts and Folklore Archives (http://www.wku. edu/Library/disc/)

FOLKLORE JOURNALS

Three of the journals listed here, the *Journal of American Folklore, Folklore,* and *Western Folklore,* can be accessed through the journal storage website JSTOR (http://www.jstor.org).

American Journal of Play (http://www.americanjournalofplay.org)

Children's Folklore Review (http://www.ecu.edu/english/journals/)

Contemporary Legend (http://www.panam.edu/faculty/mglazer/isclr/Contemporary Legend.htm)

Culture and Tradition (http://www.ucs.mun.ca/~culture)

Folklore (http://www.tandf.co.uk/journals/titles/0015587X.asp)

Folklore Fellows Communications (http://www.folklorefellows.org)

Folklore Forum (https://www.indiana.edu/~folkpub/forum)

Journal of American Folklore (http://www.afsnet.org/publications/jaf/cfm)

Journal of Folklore Research (http://www.indiana.edu/~jofr)

Play and Folklore (http://www.museumvictoria.com.au/About/Books-and-Journals/Play-and-Folklore/)

Voices: The Journal of New York Folklore (http://www.nyfolklore.org/pubs/newpub.html)

Western Folklore (http://www.westernfolklore.org/WesternFolklore.htm)

CHILDREN'S MUSEUMS

Boston Children's Museum, Massachusetts (http://www.bostonchildrensmuseum.org)

Children's Museum of Indianapolis (http://www.childrensmuseum.org)

Istanbul Toy Museum, Turkey (http://www.istanbuloyuncakmuzesi.com/eng/default.asp)

National Children's Museum (http://www.ccm.org)

Strong National Museum of Play, Rochester, New York (http://www.museumofplay.org)

Victoria and Albert Museum of Childhood, London, England (http://www.museumofchildhood.org.uk)

Yokohama Doll Museum, Japan (http://www.welcome.city.yokohama.jp/eng/doll/4000.html)

SELECTED CHILDREN'S FOLKLORE WEB SITES

Children's Folklore Section, American Folklore Society (http://www.afsnet.org/sections/children/)

Children's Studies, York University, Canada (http://www.yorku.ca/web/futurestudents/programs/template.asp?Id=639)

City Lore (http://www.citylore.org)

Cocojams (http://cocojams.com)

Folkstreams: The Best of American Folklore Films (http://www.folkstreams.net)

National Children's Folksong Repository (http://www.edu-cyberpg.com/NCFR/NCFR.html)

Streetplay.com (http://www.streetplay.com)

Index

About the Author

ELIZABETH TUCKER is Professor of English at Binghamton University. Her previous books include *Campus Legends: A Handbook* (Greenwood, 2005).